**Fikadu Goshu**

# Sectoral Analysis of the Impact of Foreign Aid on Economic Growth in Ethiopia

## Time Series Analysis of Agriculture, Education and Health Sectors

Anchor Academic
Publishing

**Goshu, Fikadu: Sectoral Analysis of the Impact of Foreign Aid on Economic Growth in Ethiopia: Time Series Analysis of Agriculture, Education and Health Sectors, Hamburg, Anchor Academic Publishing 2015**

Buch-ISBN: 978-3-95489-358-4
PDF-eBook-ISBN: 978-3-95489-858-9
Druck/Herstellung: Anchor Academic Publishing, Hamburg, 2015

**Bibliografische Information der Deutschen Nationalbibliothek:**
Die Deutsche Nationalbibliothek verzeichnet diese Publikation in der Deutschen Nationalbibliografie; detaillierte bibliografische Daten sind im Internet über http://dnb.d-nb.de abrufbar.

**Bibliographical Information of the German National Library:**
The German National Library lists this publication in the German National Bibliography. Detailed bibliographic data can be found at: http://dnb.d-nb.de


Hermannstal 119k, 22119 Hamburg
http://www.diplomica-verlag.de, Hamburg 2015
Printed in Germany

**Acknowledgment**

First and for most I would thank the Almighty God for his an invaluable helps for all things that human beings can perform with help of his supreme power.

Then, I would like to express my sincere gratitude to my advisor Dr Amsalu Bedemo (PhD) and Mr Wondimu Saketa (MSc) for their genuine and constructive ideas of providing their comments and their patience to go through and forward comments with respect to the work of research work on the title of sectoral analysis of the effect of foreign aid in Ethiopia.

My special thanks would be extended to Mekonnen Bersisa (PhD Candidate), who has given me a genuine and constructive comments starting from the modification of the title by sharing from the meager time he has for his personal study.

Last but not list, I have a great full thanks to my wife S/r Deme Chemeda, my sister Adanech Iteffa and others for their support and taking care of our children Firomsa Fikadu and Bilise Fikadu during my research work and reviewing of different sources for this interesting work.

## Table of Content

## Acronyms

| | |
|---|---|
| AIC | Akakie Information Criteria |
| ADF | Augmented Dickey-Fuller |
| DAC | Development Assistance Committee |
| ECT | Error Correction Term |
| GBS | General Budget Support |
| GCF | Gross Capital Formation |
| GDP | Gross Domestic Product |
| GNI | Gross National Income |
| EPRDF | Ethiopian Peoples' Revolutionary Democratic Front |
| IMF | International Monetary Fund |
| LDCs | Least Developed Countries |
| MoFED | Ministry of Finance and Economic Development |
| NGO | Non Governmental Organization |
| ODA | Official Development Assistance |
| OECD | Organization for Economic Cooperation and Development |
| OLS | Ordinary List Square |
| SSA | Sub-Sahara Africa |
| UNCTAD | United Nations Conference on Trade and Development |
| VAR | Vector Auto regression |
| VECM | Vector Error Correction Model |
| WB | World Bank |
| WIDER | World Institute for Development Economics Research |

## List of Table

## List of Figure

## Abstract

*This study has examined sectoral analysis of the impact of foreign aid on aggregate and sectoral economic growth in Ethiopia over the period 1981 to 2012 using Multivariate Vector Auto Regression analysis. All the necessary time series tests such as stationary test, co-integration test, weak exiguity test, vector error correction, and causality test in vector error correction model and the like are conducted. The empirical result from the growth equation shows that aid has a significant positive impact on educational sector GDP growth in the long run. On the other hand, foreign aid has positive but insignificant impact on real GDP growth, agriculture GDP growth, and health sector GDP growth of Ethiopia for the period under consideration. Foreign aid is effective in enhancing economic growth at aggregate level of Ethiopia in general and education sector in particular. The result of the study reveals that there is a bi-directional causal relationship between educational GDP and educational foreign aid in Ethiopia. There is also a unidirectional causality between agricultural aid and agricultural GDP growth. However, the health sector does not show any causality with their respective sector aid. This implies that aid allocated for certain sectors is ineffective in achieving its objectives of economic growth. Therefore, aid recipient country like Ethiopia has to work how to enhance the domestic revenue raising capacity of the country which is at the heart of the mechanism to meet the capital required for the economy in times of short falls and ineffectiveness of external resources.*

***Key words:*** *foreign aid, economic growth, sectoral, aggregate, Ethiopia, impact*

# CHAPTER ONE: INTRODUCTION

## 1.1. Background

Developing countries face challenges of massive poverty, slow Gross Domestic Product (GDP) growth, high mortality rates from illnesses, and low levels of education. More than 20 percent of the developing world (1.1 billion) people subsist on less than $1 a day. In some developing countries, such as those of Sub-Saharan Africa (SSA), more than 70 percent of the population lives in extreme poverty (i.e. the proportion of population earning less than $2 a day) (Kumler'07, 2007; Leeson, 2008). The governments in these countries do not have sufficient financial resources to fight these challenges effectively. Foreign aid has played an instrumental role in the implementation of development programs to combat the challenges (Lohani'04, 2004; Pattillo, Polak, & Roy, 2007).

Foreign aid is defined as any flow of capital to a developing countries for the objective that should be non commercial from the point of view of the donor on development, poverty reduction, or income distribution grounds and it should be characterized by concessional terms; that is, the interest rate and repayment period for borrowed capital should be softer (less stringent) than commercial terms (Bakare, 2011; Randhawa, 2012; Todaro & Smith, 2012). Official Development Assistance (ODA), commonly known as foreign aid is a flow of financial resources from developed countries to developing countries on development grounds (Eroglu & Yavaz, 2005; Moreira, 2005; Leeson, 2008; Paul & Pistor, 2009). It is an international transfer of public funds in the form of loans or grants either directly from one government to another (bilateral) or indirectly through multilateral assistance agency such as International Monetary Fund and World Bank (Radelet, 2006; UNCTAD, 2006; Abuzeid, 2009; OECD, 2009).

Similarly, Development Assistance Committee (DAC) defines ODA as a grants or loans to developing countries and multilateral agencies active in development that are undertaken by the official sector at concessional terms (if a loan, having a grant element of at least 25%), with the promotion of economic development and welfare as the main objective. Technical cooperation is also included in aid. Grants, loans, and credits to be used in military purposes are excluded (OECD, 2009; Paul & Pistor, 2009).

Despite the volume of ODA from bilateral and multilateral agency flows has grown from an annual rate of under $5 billion in 1960 to $50 billion in 2000 and then to over $128 billion in 2008, the percentage of developed country Gross National Income (GNI) allocated to ODA declined from 0.51 percent in 1960 to 0.23 percent in 2002 before improving to 0.33 percent by 2005 and then to 0.45 percent in 2008 as part of a campaign to increase assistance in the wake of the continued lag in human development in Sub-Saharan Africa (OECD, 2009; Paul & Pistor, 2009; Todaro & Smith, 2012).

Foreign aid is important source of finance in most countries in SSA where it supplements low savings, narrow export earnings and thin tax bases (Bhattarai, 2007; Arellano, Bulíř, Lane, & Lipschitz, 2009). Africa in general and SSA in particular receives a greater share of global aid than any other region in the world with East Africa receiving approximately 25 percent of all ODA to SSA. Within East Africa, Ethiopia receives the largest percentage (7%) of total ODA from all donors, followed by Tanzania (6%). According to OECD DAC statistics, aid to Ethiopia increased from US$1.1 billion in 1995 to US$3.5 billion in 2010 and is concentrated on core social sectors and infrastructure (Nganwa, 2013; Prizzon & Rogerson, 2013).

Most foreign aid is designed to meet one or more of broad economic and development objectives: to stimulate economic growth through building infrastructure, supporting productive sectors such as agriculture, or bringing new ideas and technologies; to strengthen education, health, environmental, or political systems; to support subsistence consumption of food and other commodities, especially during relief operations or humanitarian crises; or to help stabilize an economy following economic shocks (WB, 1998; Radelet, 2006; Bakare, 2011).

## 1.2. Statement of the Problem

Despite these broader objectives of foreign aid as well as the tremendous increases in the follow of foreign aid to developing countries like Ethiopia (under $5 billion in 1960 to $50 billion in 2000 and to over $128 billion in 2008) (OECD, 2009) from time to time, there is controversies about aid effectiveness which go back to decades. There are two general but contending schools of thought with regard to the effectiveness of aid in spurring economic growth in the third world (Gebhard, Kitterman, Mitchell, Nielson, & Wilson, 2008). Research results on the macroeconomic impacts of foreign aid in developing countries are ambiguous. Some studies concluded that this relationship was negative; others concluded it was positive, and others found no relationship at all. Several studies have noted that foreign aid has a positive effect on the economic growth of poor countries (Chenery & Strout, 1966; Burnside & Dollar, 2000; Lohani'04, 2004; Bhattarai, 2007).

Foreign aid is advocated the promotion of economic development and could play a vital role in promoting economic development in the Less Developed Countries (LDCs) which is explained in term of concepts such as the savings gap and the foreign exchange gap (Eroglu & Yavaz, 2005; Shah, Ahmad, & Zahid, 2005).

Critics of foreign aid argue that foreign aid discourages domestic saving and domestic tax revenue in developing countries and is simply diverted into consumption instead of investment. They find that grant have a negative effect on domestic revenue. The decline domestic revenue is almost as much as the increase in grant (Benedek, Crivelli, Gupta, & Muthoora, 2012; Bwire, Morrissey, & Lloyda, 2013). Since these countries do not have the technical ability to use the aid effectively, it gets spent on nonproductive activities and poorly conceived projects concluding that there exists no significant correlation between aid and GDP growth because the majority of foreign aid is spent on consumption (Lohani'04, 2004).

The study of foreign aid on a sectoral basis that is conducted by cross country analysis doesn't allow us to clearly examine the sectoral impact of aid on sector's spending. In this respect, different countries have different result for the impact of aid on sectors spending (Paul & Pistor, 2009). Projects financed by foreign aid are often highly visible and important successes such as roads and highways, schools and health clinics, irrigation infrastructure, power plants and so on. But success can be assessed at two levels that are at the micro or project level, which typically shows high rates of success or at the macro level of economy wide growth and poverty reduction, where there is less visible success (WB, 1998; Pettersson, 2007). Generally, there seemed to be a micro–macro paradox, with evidence suggested that aid clearly worked at the micro level but evidence, on balance, relating to the macro level (McGillivray, Feeny, Hermes, & Lensink, 2005; Odusanya, Abidemi, & Akanni, 2011).

Odusanya et al (2011) carried out studies on the impact of foreign aid and public expenditure on economic growth in Nigeria. Their result reveals that foreign aid and public expenditure impact positively on the economic growth with foreign aid indicating a very significant impact on growth. They conclude that foreign aid can have positive effect on economic growth, through public expenditure if properly channeled to the productive sectors of the economy. But Odusanya et al (2011) carried out their studies using static framework. Their conclusions may be incorrect because the economic agents associated with aid administration are dynamic. Also, they did not disaggregate the GDP into different sector levels for the sectoral level study they have conducted. Therefore, this research tends to use dynamic model that capture the dynamic nature of these agencies.

Also, for the analysis of sectoral level, this study used sectoral level GDP instead of aggregate GDP. Hence, such work can usually be conducted in the context of country specific, to capture the different impact of earmarked aid on the sectors. It is therefore pertinent to check whether and to what extent has foreign aid might have caused or contributed to economic growth in Ethiopia.

## 1.3. Objective of the Study

### 1.3.1. General Objectives

The major objective of the study is to investigate sectoral analysis of the impact of foreign aid on economic growth in Ethiopia.

### 1.3.2. Specific Objectives

The specific objectives of the study are to:

- Analyze the trend of macroeconomic performance of Ethiopia under two regime so as to draw implications for economic growth;
- Analysis the causality between foreign aid and economic growth both at aggregate and sectoral level;
- Analyze the impact of foreign aid on aggregate agriculture, education and health sector economic growth in Ethiopia.

## 1.4. Research Questions

The above specific objectives can be met by answering the following research questions.

- What were the trends of macroeconomic performance of Ethiopia in the past and the then government regime?
- What is the causal relationship that exists between foreign aid and economic growth at aggregate and sectoral in Ethiopia?
- What is the impact of foreign aid on economic growth of developmental sectors?
- In which sectors of the economy does foreign aid has significant effect?

## 1.5. Hypothesis to be Tested

This study is inspired by a new stream of researches that supports aid works better at sectoral level (micro level) in an individual country based study than at cross country level (macro-level). Specifically the main hypotheses to be empirically tested are:

1. There is no any relationship between economic growth and foreign aid in the two regimes in Ethiopia.
2. Foreign aid does not Granger-cause GDP growth for aggregate and sectoral GDP of Ethiopia in the past and the present government.
3. Sectoral foreign aid does not have an impact on sectoral economic growth of agriculture, health and education.

## 1.6. Significance of the Study

The study of sectoral analysis of the impact of foreign aid in Ethiopia is important due to the fact that foreign aid may have differentiated impacts at the sector levels as compared to the results obtained when analyzed at an aggregate level. It is noteworthy that the impact of foreign aid at the sectoral level has not been given consideration in analysis of impact of foreign aid in Ethiopia at large. Therefore, the result of this study is useful for improving policy design, institutional set up, implementation, monitoring and evaluation in the area of foreign aid allocation to public spending in general and sector wise in particular for the sake of economic growth. Finally, the result of the study with respect to sectoral analysis of foreign aid becomes stepping stone for academicians, researchers, students, policy makers and other organization that are in need to use its result as an input in their organization.

## 1.7. Scope and Limitation of the Study

### 1.7.1. Scope of the Study

This study covers a period of thirty two years for a country level data analysis in Ethiopia. The study uses aggregate foreign aid; sectoral level foreign aid of agriculture, education and health; government spending on aggregate, agriculture, education, and health sectors; aggregate GDP, health, agriculture, and educational GDP of Ethiopia and other time series data of the period of 1981 to 2012 is used in the analysis.

### 1.7.2. Limitation of the Study

The model used in the analysis of the impact of foreign aid in Ethiopia assumes that all aid is allocated through government sector and none of it will be spend though other ways. This is due to the fact that in developing countries like Ethiopia, aid may have come through Non-Governmental Organizations (NGO) or other sources that are understate the whole figure of aid that is used in the study for the period.

The other critical limitation of this study is that in the analysis of aid flows to sectors with recipient's country wise in the context of the total aid flow during the past three or more decades is greatly hampered by the lack of complete, reliable, and consistent data. To the best of my knowledge, the only systematic data available and easily accessible for researcher is foreign aid flows that have been compiled by the OECD/DAC. However, the easily accessible OECD/DAC website does not provide a consistent and comparable breakdown of aid flows from both multilateral and bilateral donors from the early 1970s to the present. This source provides a sectoral classification of aid flows from the 1973 onward only for the bilateral aid and not for the rest of foreign aid from the donors.

Furthermore, the sectoral classification of the total aid flows to individual country like Ethiopia is available only from 1995 to 2012 that the researcher used in the study. Moreover, the data available regarding aid to the sector from the OCED/DAC database has a category of "multi-sectoral" aid which includes aid to more than one sector. Therefore, it is not clear for researcher how much aid from multi-sectoral aid is directly or indirectly goes to which sector of the economy in recipient countries in general and to agriculture, health and education sectors in particular. This also makes us to underestimate the aid allocated to agriculture, education and health sectors which are the main concerns of this study.

## 1.8. Organization of the Paper

The study of research is organized under five chapters. The first chapter deals with the problems and its approaches, which include background of the study, statement of the problem, research objectives, research questions to be answered, significance of the study, hypothesis to be tested, scope and limitation of the study, and organization of the research paper. The second chapter deals with methodology of the study that includes source and type of data, description of variables, model specification, and estimation techniques.

Chapter three deals with macroeconomic performance of the country which includes: GDP & its growth trend including per capita GDP, and the share of main economic sectors (agriculture, industry and service) in GDP; trends of gross fixed capital formation and saving of Ethiopia in the two regimes; the trends in external market (export-import) and its annual growth; and finally trends and sectoral compositions of ODA flows to Ethiopia. Chapter three also presents the estimation results and time series characteristics of the data and tests for long-run relationships and short run model. The last chapter, chapter four, gives summary, conclusions and policy implication of the study. All the reference materials consulted in the study are listed under reference. Sample of the test results are listed under the appendix section of the study.

# CHAPTER TWO: METHODOLOGY OF THE STUDY

## 2.1. Data Types and Sources of Data

Concerns of analyzing the impact of foreign aid are important for Ethiopia due to an increasing per capita of foreign aid and the country's dependence on it. The study used time series data. For analyzing the impact of foreign aid on economic growth of Ethiopia, the study used country level macro-data covering the period from 1981 to 2012. The choice of the period is based on the availability of relevant data for the study. The relevant data was collected from various sources: National Bank of Ethiopia; Ministry of Finance and Economic Development (MoFED); Ethiopian Economic Association; World Bank; World Development Indicator database; and OECD/CRS websites.

## 2.2. Description of Variables

The major variables that are used in the sectoral analysis foreign aid in Ethiopia include: Real GDP which is the real GDP of an economy over the period 1981-2012 for Ethiopia both at aggregate and at sectoral level for agriculture, health and education which are dependent variables. Furthermore, AGDP is agricultural GDP, EDGDP is educational GDP; and HEGDP is health sector GDP of the country that are used in the analysis. FAID is the ODA as defined by the OECD as percentage of GDP. Also EDUCAID, AGRIAID, and HEALAID are official development assistance allocated for educational, agriculture and health sector as percentage of GDP of the country respectively.

PRIV is the total net private capital flows as a percentage of GDP (international remittance can also be classified as part of net private capital flows). Private capital flows consist of net foreign direct investment and portfolio investment. SAV is the domestic savings as a percentage of GDP. TRADE is the openness to trade, which is defined as (X + M) /GDP. That is the addition of export and import divided by GDP. Openness to trade is often hypothesized to raise growth through several channels, such as access to advanced technology from abroad, possibilities of catch-up, greater access to a variety of inputs for production, and access to broader markets that raise the efficiency of domestic production through increased specialization. Various measures of openness have been proposed and tested, with no single 'best' measure emerging. For instance, (Durbarry, Gemmell, & Greenaway, 1998) used to measure trade openness by the ratio of total trade to GDP and changes in the terms of trade. X is total value of goods and services exported and M is total value of goods and services imported. Moreover, GOV represents the total amount of government expenditure (developmental plus non developmental) as a percentage of GDP for the period under consideration.

D is dummy variable for major political changes from Derg regime to Ethiopian peoples' Revolutionary Democratic Front (EPRDF) that takes in to account to see the effect of major shifts in political environment on the performance of economic growth and foreign aid in the short run. The dummies are incorporated in to the model for growth and D took 1 for 1992 to 2012 and 0 otherwise.

## 2.3. Model Specification

Different researcher uses different models. This study employs Vector Autoregressive (VAR) model. One of the main advantages of VAR model over single equation model is that its ability to deal with several endogenous variables(Hayakawa, 2011) and cointegrating vectors, the ability to test for weak exogeneity and parameter restrictions, and to handle both I(1) and I(0) variables in one system. The VAR approach is data based and little economic theory is imposed directly (M'Amanja, Lloyd, & Morrissey, 2005). VAR assumes that all the variables are endogenous.

The model used in this study was rely on the framework of Durbarry, et al (1998) as modified by Odusanya et al (2011) for the case of Nigeria. However, in order to meet the objectives of study in terms of its concentration, as well as on the bases of availability of data on the appropriate variables, foreign aid, total private capital flows, and domestic saving mobilized as a vector of capital sources (domestic and foreign), and openness to trade and total government expenditure as is a vector of control variables from economic growth components over the other variables to capture potential side effects of foreign aid such as 'Dutch-Disease' effects and other policy variables that are hypothesized to affect growth are incorporated (Odusanya, Abidemi, & Akanni, 2011). It was hypothesized that economy growth can be related to foreign aid as:

$$Growth = \beta_0 + \beta_1 FAID + \beta_2 PRIV + \beta_3 SAV + \beta_4 TRADE + \beta_5 GOV + e \ldots\ldots\ldots\ldots (1)$$

Where: Growth is the real GDP over the period 1981-2012 for Ethiopia;

FAID is the foreign aid (net ODA) flows as percentage of GDP;

PRIV is the total net private capital flows as a percentage of GDP;

SAV is the domestic savings as a percentage of GDP;

TRADE is the openness to trade, which is defined as (X + M) /GDP;

GOV is the total amount of government expenditure as a percentage of GDP.

However, in order to concentrate on the dynamic effect of foreign aid on the economic growth at the sectoral levels, equation 1 is first modified to VAR model as:

$$FA_t = \beta_0 + \sum_{j=1}^{p} \beta_{1j} FA_{it-j} + \sum_{j=1}^{p} \beta_{2j} AG_{it-j} + l_{it} \ldots\ldots\ldots\ldots\ldots\ldots\ldots\ldots\ldots\ldots\ldots\ldots (2)$$

$$AG_t = a_0 + \sum_{j=1}^{p} a_{1j}\, AG_{it-j} + \sum_{j=1}^{p} a_{2j} FA_{it-j} + \mu_{it} \ldots\ldots\ldots\ldots\ldots\ldots\ldots\ldots\ldots\ldots\ldots\ldots (3)$$

Where *FA* and *AG* are foreign aid and annual GDP growth respectively, while $FA_{t-j}$ and $AG_{t-j}$ represent their lagged values in *j* years, *p* is the maximum lag length. That is, the Lag Exclusion Wald Tests will be used to select the most appropriate lag length, and $\ell$ and μ are error terms and, β's and *a*'s are parameters to be estimated.

Differencing away the fixed effects in equation 2 and 3 by including TRADE, GOV and D (D is dummy variable) it was transformed to equations 4 and 5 respectively which will be used to examine the impact of foreign aid on the Ethiopian economy at the aggregate level. Where Δ denotes the first difference operator, $\eta_i$ *and* $\zeta_i$ are random error terms.

$$\Delta FA_t = \beta_0 + \sum_{j=1}^{p} \beta_{1j} \Delta FA_{it-j} + \sum_{j=1}^{p} \beta_{2j} \Delta AG_{it-j} + \sum_{j=1}^{2} \delta_j D_{it-j} + \sum_{j=1}^{p} \delta_j\, GOV_{it-j} + \sum_{j=1}^{p} \gamma_j\, TRADE_{it-j} + \eta_i . (4)$$

$$\Delta AG_t = a_0 + \sum_{j=1}^{p} a_{1j}\, \Delta AG_{it-j} + \sum_{j=1}^{p} a_{2j} \Delta FA_{it-j} + \sum_{j=1}^{2} \delta_j D_{it-j} + \sum_{j=1}^{p} \delta_j\, GOV_{it-j} + \sum_{j=1}^{p} \gamma_j\, TRADE_{it-j} + \zeta_i . (5)$$

In the sectoral analysis, the impact of foreign aid on agriculture, health and education will be analyzed. Going by equations 4 and 5, FA will be the foreign aid for agriculture, health and education respectively, while AG will be the agriculture, health, and educational sector GDP growth respectively for the period under consideration in the sectoral analysis.

## 2.4. Econometric Estimation Techniques

The method employed in the study is based on recent advancements in the theoretical and empirical aid-growth relationships. As the data used is time series, testing for stationarity (unit root test), co-integration test, Vector Error Correction Model (VECM), and causality test is conducted in the model. The standard estimation and hypothesis testing assumed that all, in particular regression, variables are stationary. A data series is said to be stationary if its error term has zero mean, constant variance and the covariance between any two time periods depends only on the distance or lag between the two periods and not on the actual time which it is computed.

However in reality most macroeconomic variables are non stationary. If variables entering into the estimation are non stationary, then the result obtained using OLS technique would be spurious in the sense that variables would seem to have promising diagnostic test (high $R^2$ and low Durbin Watson test) result just because they have common trend over time rather than actual causation(Harris, 1995). Therefore hypothesis testing and inference using such results will be invalid. To avoid such wrong inferences from the non stationary regressions, the time series property of the data should be checked prior to the estimation of the long run model.

### 2.4.1. Testing for Unit Root

Unit root test has become a widely popular approach to test for stationary. It has been argued that if a variable has deterministic trend, including trend variable in the regression removes the trend component and makes it stationary. Such process is called trend stationary since the deviation from the trend is stationary. However, most time series data have a characteristic of stochastic trend (that is, the trend is variable cannot be predicted with certainty). In such cases, in order to avoid the problem associated with spurious regression, pre-testing the variables for the existence of unit roots (i.e. non-stationary) becomes compulsory. In general if a variable has stochastic trend, it needs to be differenced in order to obtain stationary. Such process is called difference stationary process (Gujarati D. , 1995). The number of unit roots a given variable posses determines how many times that variable should be differenced in order to attain stationary.

A commonly applied formal test for existence of a unit root in the data is the Dickey-Fuller (DF) tests. It's simple extension being the Augmented Dickey Fuller (ADF) test. The augmentation is adding lagged values (p) of first differences of the dependent variable as additional regressors which are required to account for possible occurrence of autocorrelation. The Dickey-Fuller test starts with the following first order autoregressive model:

$$Y_t = \phi Y_{t-1} + U_t \ldots\ldots\ldots\ldots\ldots\ldots\ldots\ldots\ldots\ldots\ldots\ldots\ldots\ldots(6)$$

Subtracting $Y_{t-1}$ from both sides gives

$$\Delta Y_t = \gamma Y_{t-1} + U_t \quad where\ \gamma = (\phi - 1), U_t \sim IID\ (0, \delta^2) \ldots\ldots\ldots\ldots\ldots\ldots(7)$$

Then the test for stationarity is conducted on the parameter γ. If γ=0 or δ=1 it implies that the variable Y is not stationary. The hypothesis to be tested is formulated as follows:

Ho: γ=0 or δ=1

H1: γ < 0 or δ< 0

Furthermore, the use of equation (7) is appropriate only when the series $Y_t$ has a zero mean and no trend term (Harris, 1995). If a variable has a zero mean, it implies that $Y_t$= 0 when t=0 implying no constant term. A constant (drift) is included to the regression since it is difficult to know whether the true value of $Y_0$ is zero or not. Including a constant (α) to equation (7) gives:

$$\Delta Y_t = \alpha + \gamma Y_{t-1} + U_t \ldots\ldots\ldots\ldots\ldots\ldots\ldots\ldots\ldots\ldots\ldots\ldots\ldots\ldots(8)$$

However, testing for stationarity using equation (8) is invalid if a series contains a deterministic trend. Because if γ=0, the null hypothesis will be accepted that the series contains a stochastic trend when there exists deterministic trend. Thus to avoid such results, it is important to incorporate time trend in the equation above and gives:

$$\Delta Y_t = \alpha + \gamma Y_{t-1} + \beta T + U_t \ldots\ldots\ldots\ldots\ldots\ldots\ldots\ldots\ldots\ldots\ldots\ldots\ldots(9)$$

Where, T the trend element

For the above equations (equation 8 and 9), the parameter $\gamma$ is used while testing for stationarity and the decision is made using t-statistics that is used for the regression without drift and trend. If the calculated value of t is less than the critical value the null hypothesis is accepted and not if otherwise. Accepting the null hypothesis implies the presence of unit root- i.e. the series is non stationary. However, the DF test has a series limitation in that it suffers from residual autocorrelation. Therefore to overcome this problem, the DF model is augmented with additional lagged first differences of the dependent variable. This is called Augmented Dickey-Fuller model.

The advantage of using ADF over that of DF model is that ADF model avoids the autocorrelation among the residuals. Therefore incorporating lagged first differences of the dependent variable to the above three equations (equations 7, 8 and 9) gives the corresponding ADF model as follows:

$$\Delta Y_t = \gamma Y_{t-1} + + \sum_{i-1}^{k} \theta_i \Delta Y_{t-i} + \varepsilon_t \ldots\ldots\ldots (10)$$

$$\Delta Y_t = \alpha + \gamma Y_{t-1} + + \sum_{i-1}^{k} \theta_i \Delta Y_{t-i} + \varepsilon_t \ldots\ldots\ldots (11)$$

$$\Delta Y_t = \alpha + \beta T + \gamma Y_{t-1} + + \sum_{i-1}^{k} \theta_i \Delta Y_{t-i} + \varepsilon_t \ldots\ldots\ldots (12)$$

Where, $Y_t$ is any variable in the model to be tested for stationarity, $\alpha$ is a constant (drift), T is a trend element, k is the lag length, $\varepsilon_t$ is an error term, and $\Delta$ is the first difference operator.

The null hypothesis of ADF is $\delta=0$ against alternative hypothesis that $\delta<0$. Where $\delta=\gamma-1$. A rejection of this hypothesis means that the time series is stationary or it does not contains a unit root while not rejecting means that the time series is non stationary(Enders, 1995). If the variable that is not stationary in levels appear to be stationary after $d^{th}$ difference, then the variable is said to be integrated of order d I(d).

### 2.4.2. Test for Cointegration

Before going to examine the causal relationship between aid and economic growth, it is better to check whether the two variables are cointegrating or not. Cointegration means the regressions of one variable over the other is no meaning full (spurious). Economically speaking, two variables will be cointegrated if they have a long-term, or equilibrium, relationship between them (Gujarati D. , 2004). Despite variables are being individually non stationary, a linear combination of two or more time series can be stationary. Cointegration among the variables reflects the presence of long run relationship among non stationary variables in the system.

Testing for cointegration is important because differencing the variables to attain stationarity generates a model that does not show long run behavior of the variables. Thus testing for cointegration is the same as testing for long run relationship. In general, if variables that are integrated of order'd' produce a linear combination which is integrated of order less than 'd' say 'b', then the variables are cointegrated and hence have long run relationship(Gujarati D. , 2004). In order to determine whether or not a long-run equilibrium relationship exists among the unit root variables in a given model, we need to test empirically that the series in the model are cointegrated. To conduct test for co-integration, the study used Johanson (1988) maximum likelihood estimation procedure.

To conduct a test for co-integration in a multivariate framework using Johansen's maximum likelihood procedure, first the general VAR model of relationship between the variables should have to be formulated. Thus a general VAR (p) of the following form is formulated:

$$X_t = \phi_1 X_{t-1} + \phi_2 X_{t-2} + \cdots + \phi_p X_{t-p} + \Psi W_t + \varepsilon_t \ldots\ldots\ldots\ldots\ldots\ldots\ldots\ldots\ldots\ldots\ldots\ldots\ldots (13)$$

Where $X_t$ is a (mx1) vector of stochastic I(1) variables, $W_t$ is a (qx1) vector of deterministic variables (for instance trend and dummy variables), and each $\phi_i$ (i=1....p) and $\Psi$ are (mxm) and (mxq) matrices of parameters. $\varepsilon_t$ is a (mx1) vector of normally and independently distributed disturbances with zero mean and non-diagonal covariance matrix (vector of white noise disturbance terms), and t=1....T (T is the number of observation).

Providing the variables are (at most) integrated of order one i.e. I(1) and co-integrated also has an equilibrium error correction representation that is observationally equivalent but which facilitates estimation and hypothesis testing, as all terms are stationary. The vector error correction model (VECM) is:

$$\Delta X_t = \pi X_{t-p} + \Gamma_1 \Delta X_{t-1} + \Gamma_2 \Delta X_{t-2} + \cdots + \Gamma_{p-1} \Delta X_{t-p-1} + \Psi W_t + \varepsilon_t \ldots\ldots\ldots\ldots\ldots (14)$$

Simplifying equation (14) gives:

$$\Delta X_t = \sum_{i=1}^{p-1} \Tau_i \Delta X_{t-i} + \pi X_{t-p} + \Psi W_t + \varepsilon_t \ldots\ldots (15)$$

Where, i= 1-------p-1, $\tau_i = -[I - \sum_{j=i+1}^{p} \phi_j]$ and $\pi = -[I - \sum_{j=1}^{p} \phi_j]$

From the above equation, the long run relationship among the variables is captured by the term $\pi X_{t-p}$. The $\tau_i$ coefficients estimate the short run effects of shocks on $\Delta X_t$ and thereby allow the short and long run responses to differ. In the Johansen (1988) procedure, determining the rank of π (i.e. the maximum number of linearly independent stationary columns in π) provides the number of cointegrating vector between the elements in x. In this connection, there are three cases worth mentioning. (i), If the rank of π is zero it points that the matrix is null which means that the variables are not co-integrated. In such case the above model is used in first difference, with no long run information,( ii), If the rank of π equals the number of variables in the system (say n) then π has full rank which implies that the vector process is stationary. Therefore the VAR can be tested in levels, (iii), If π has a reduced rank i. e. $1<r(\pi)<n$ it suggests that there exists $r<(n-1)$ cointegrating vector where r is the number of co-integration in the system.

The matrix π is given by ($\pi=\alpha\beta'$), where β coefficients show the long run relationship between the variables in the system(Cointegration parameters) and α coefficients show the amount of changes in the variables to bring the system back to equilibrium i.e. it shows the speed with which disequilibrium from the long run path is adjusted. To identify the number of cointegrating vectors, the Johansen procedure provides n eigenvalues (λ) characteristic roots whose magnitude measures the degree of correlation of the cointegration relations with the stationary elements in the model.

Two test statistics ($\lambda_{trace}$ and $\lambda_{max}$) are used to test the number of cointegrating vectors, based on the characteristic roots. The statistics are calculated from the following formula:

$$\lambda_{trace} = -T \sum_{i=r+1}^{n} \ln(1 - \hat{\lambda}_i), r = 0, 1, \ldots . n - 1 \ldots\ldots (16)$$

$$\lambda_{max} = -T(1 - \hat{\lambda}_{r+1}) \ldots\ldots (17)$$

Where, T the sample size, $\lambda_\iota$ is the estimated eigenvalues

In Johanson procedure, the likelihood ratio (LR) test is used to test the significance of estimates of $\lambda_i$ eigenvalues. The $\lambda_{trace}$ tests the null that the number of co-integrating vectors is less than or equal to r against an alternative of (r+1). The $\lambda_{max}$ statistics, on the other hand, tests the null that the number of co-integrating vectors is r against an alternative of (r+1). The distribution of both test statistics follows chi-square distribution.

Since the VAR approach assumes that all variables in the system are potentially endogenous, it is important to identify the endogenous and exogenous variables in the system. M'Amanja, Lloyd & Morrissey (2005) pointed that the weak exogeneity test gives an indication of the variables in the system with feedback effects on the long run levels of other variables but themselves are not influenced by these long run variables (M'Amanja, Lloyd, & Morrissey, 2005). This implies that if a variable is weakly exogenous its error correction term doesn't enter the error correction model. As a result the dynamic growth equation for that variable depicts no information concerning the long run relationship in the system. Thus such variables should appear in the right hand side of the VECM. For this reason test for weak exogeneity is conducted by imposing zero restriction on the relevant adjustment parameters.

### 2.4.3 Vector Error Correction Model

Obtaining long-run estimates of cointegration relationships is only a first step to estimating the complete model. The short-run structure of the model is also important in terms of the information it conveys on the short run adjustment behavior of economic variables. The analysis of short-run dynamics is often done by first eliminating trends in the variables, usually by differencing. This procedure, however, throws away potential valuable information about long-run relationships about which economic theories have a lot to say.

Vector error correction model enables to capture the short run dynamics of the model and formulated based on the identified long run relationships. The VECM has cointegration relation built into the specification so that it restricts the long run behavior of the endogenous variable to converge to their cointegrating relationships while allowing for short run adjustment dynamics. The cointegrating term is known as the error correction term since the deviation from long run equilibrium is corrected gradually through a series of partial short run adjustments. Thus cointegration implies the presence of error correcting representation and any deviation from equilibrium will revert back to its long run path.

The existence of co-integration allows for the analysis of the short run dynamic model that identifies adjustment to the long run equilibrium relationship through the error correction model representation. If the number of co-integrating vector(s) is/are determined and once the endogenous and exogenous variables are identified in the system, it is possible to formulate a VECM. Using the variables of our interest in the model a system of equations is developed that portray the VECM. Hence, assuming that $Y_t$ is endogenous variable(s) and $X_{jt}$ representing weakly exogenous variables in the model, we can model $Y_t$. $Y_t$ is modeled using the lagged first difference of $Y_t$ itself, the lagged first differences of the explanatory variables and the error correcting term which is designed to capture the speed of adjustment to the long run equilibrium. The equation is represented as:

$$\Delta Y_t = \sum_{i=0}^{p} \theta_i \, \Delta Y_{t-i} + \sum_{i=1}^{p} \alpha_i \Delta X_{jt-i} + \delta ECT_{t-1} + \lambda_i D \ldots\ldots\ldots\ldots\ldots\ldots\ldots\ldots\ldots\ldots\ldots\ldots (18)$$

Where $ECT_{t-1}$ is the error correcting term, $\Delta X_{jt-1}$ is a vector of first differences of explanatory variables, $\Delta Y_t$ is a vector of first differences of endogenous variable(s) and D is a dummy variable for major political changes. The general VECM model for growth is represented below using the respective variables used in the estimation of the long run equilibrium equation. The general VECM model for economic growth equation is specified as:

$$\Delta RGDP = \sum_{i=1}^{2} \Delta RGDP + \sum_{i=0}^{2} \Delta FAID + \sum_{i=0}^{2} \Delta PRIV + \sum_{i=0}^{2} \Delta SAV + \sum_{i=0}^{2} \Delta TRADE + \sum_{i=0}^{2} \Delta GOV + ECT_{t-1} + D \ldots\ldots\ldots\ldots\ldots\ldots\ldots\ldots\ldots\ldots\ldots\ldots\ldots\ldots\ldots (19)$$

Where lag length of two is determined by Akakie Information Criterion (AIC), D and ECT represents a dummy for major political changes and error correction term respectively.

Using the above VECM specifications, a short run dynamic equation is estimated for growth. Dropping insignificant regressors from the specification (i.e. step-by-step elimination of insignificant regressors and lags from the general VECM model) following the general to specific modeling strategy, a parsimonious result for growth is estimated. In the estimation of the dynamic equation for growth, a dummy variable is incorporated to capture the influence of major political (government) changes on growth in the short run. In other words, dummy is used to see the immediate impact of major shifts in government on economic growth.

### 2.4.4 Causality Test in Vector Error Correction Model

The idea of Granger causality as described in (Granger, 1969) is based on the principle that a cause cannot come after its effect. When variable x is affecting a variable y, addition of the past values of the former variable should increase the precision of prediction of the latter variable (Marc., 2014). A test for causality is performed on variables of interest to detect the presence and direction of causality between pairs of variables. The variables of interest are to test causality between foreign aid and economic growth at aggregate level and foreign aid and economic growth at sectoral level by estimating a VECM for each pairs of variables. Following the VECM, causality test is made to identify the presence and direction of causality. The VECM to analyze the causal relationship economic growth and foreign aid is specified as follows:

$$\Delta GDP = \sum_{i=1}^{k} \beta g_i \Delta GDP_{t-1} + \sum_{i=0}^{l} \beta a_i \Delta FAID_{t-i} + \delta X_{t-1} + \varepsilon_t \ldots\ldots\ldots\ldots\ldots\ldots (20A)$$

$$\Delta FAID = \sum_{i=1}^{k} \theta a_i \Delta FAID_{t-1} + \sum_{i=0}^{l} \theta g_i \Delta GDP_{t-i} + \gamma Y_{t-1} + \mu_t \ldots\ldots\ldots\ldots\ldots\ldots (20B)$$

Where ($\beta g_i$, $\Theta g_i$) and ($\beta a_i$, $\Theta a_i$) are coefficients of the differenced (lagged) terms of real GDP and foreign aid respectively, ($X_{t-1}$, $Y_{t-1}$) is the one period lagged error correcting term for real GDP and foreign aid respectively. And ($\varepsilon_t$, $\gamma_t$) are white noise error terms.

Causality inferences among the pairs of variables in the above models are based upon estimating the parameters of the model, subject to the predetermined number of co-integrating vectors in the system. Then hypothesis are formulated: for the real GDP equation (20A) the null hypothesis is "foreign aid does not cause GDP growth" whereas "GDP growth does not cause foreign aid" is the null for the foreign aid equation (20B). Rejection of the null of the GDP growth equation indicates the presence of causality from foreign aid to real GDP growth, or alternatively foreign aid causes Real GDP growth. Similarly, rejection of the null for the foreign aid equation points that it is GDP growth which causes foreign aid. Furthermore, the short run and long run causality can be discriminated for each equation. Absence of causality in the short run implies that the lagged coefficient values of the first difference terms of the relevant causal variable in the VECM are jointly insignificant. Whereas long run causality test is made by imposing zero restriction on the respective adjustment parameters of each equation.

Similarly, the VECM used to examine the causal relation between sectoral GDP and foreign aid allocated to sectors. The causal relation between agricultural GDP growth and agricultural sector foreign aid was examined as follow:

$$\Delta AGDP = \sum_{i=1}^{p} ag_i \Delta AGDP_{t-1} + \sum_{i=0}^{p} ba_i \Delta AGRIAID_{t-i} + \phi W_{t-1} + Z_t \ldots\ldots\ldots\ldots (21A)$$

$$\Delta AGRIFAID = \sum_{i=1}^{k} ca_i \Delta AGRIFAID_{t-1} + \sum_{i=0}^{k} dg_i \Delta AGDP_{t-i} + \Psi S_{t-1} + U_t \ldots . (21B)$$

Where ($ag_i$,$dg_i$) and ($ba_i$,$ca_i$) are coefficients of the difference (lagged) terms of agricultural GDP and foreign aid agricultural sector respectively, ($W_{t-1}$, $S_{t-1}$) is the one period lagged error correcting term for agricultural GDP and agricultural foreign aid respectively, and p and k are optimal lag lengths determined by information criteria. And (Zt, Ut) are white noise error terms.

The null hypothesis to be tested is that there is no causality between the variables in each equation whereas rejecting the null implies the presence of causality between the variables. Absence of short run causality requires that $ba_i$ to be insignificant for agricultural aid not to cause agricultural GDP and similarly, $da_i$ to be insignificant for agricultural GDP not to cause agricultural sector aid for equations (21A) and (21B) respectively. On the other hand, absence of long run causality necessitates the coefficients (W and Ψ) of the error correcting term to be zero for the respective equations. Similarly, the causal relation between health and educational GDP and foreign aid allocated for health and educational sector done by VECM respectively. The causality test between the foreign aid and economic growth i determined by using F-test to test whether lagged information on foreign aid provides any statistically significant information about GDP growth in the presence of lagged GDP. If not, foreign aid does not Granger-cause economic growth.

In the following chapter, descriptive analysis of the macroeconomic performance of Ethiopia is described followed by estimation results and discussion of econometric variables. All the estimation of the empirical results is made by the use of STATA 10 software packages.

# CHAPTER TREE: RESULTS AND DISCUSSIONS

## 3.1. Descriptive Analysis of Macroeconomic Performance in Ethiopia

Ethiopia is the second largest populous country in Africa, with an estimated population of nearly 82.9 million (in 2009) and a growth rate of 2.2 percent per year. The country is a predominantly rural and young society with 82.4 percent of then mainly living in densely populated highland areas with settlements of 481 populations per square kilometer in the same year (World Bank, 2013). The macroeconomic performances of key economic indicators are presented at glance under this section.

### 3.1.1. Analysis of Aggregate Economic Growth in Ethiopia

The performance of an economy is highly explained by the soundness of the macroeconomic policy environment, the political framework, and various institutional setup of a given country. Indeed the design of this macroeconomic policy is a reflection of the political process that the country follows. Ethiopia had two different regimes with different policies and ideologies since 1975: Derg regime (1975-1991); and EPRDF) since 1991. Economic performance in Ethiopia is highly correlated with the political framework. Before 1974, the macroeconomic policy was largely informed by a market-oriented economic system. The period 1974-1991 witnessed a centralized economic system, where the state played a major role in all spheres of economic activity. The post-Derg period (since 1991) is again taking us back to the market-oriented system of the Imperial regime.

An Ethiopian basic macroeconomic development performance indicator shows significant improvements in the last two decades than the Derg regime and the period during transition. Rebounded from the drought shock of 2002/03, Ethiopian economy has registered a sustainable double digit broad based growth between 2003/04-2008/09 indicating that the country is on the right path economic growth. The double digit growth has been sustained throughout five consecutive years averaging 11.7 percent which was higher than that of the performance of sub-Sahara African economies during the period under consideration.

According to data from the World Bank of World Development Indicator (2014), there is a significant upward improvement in the annual real GDP of Ethiopian economy in the past three decades with annual average percentage growth of 1.4 percent between1981/82-1990/91, 4.5 percent for 1991/92-2000/01, and 8.4 percent for the year between 2001/02- 2011/12. Similarly, Ethiopian real GDP annual average performance of the economy shows a significant growth from 6.18 to 15.49 $billion in the past three decades (Table 1).

**Table 1 : Average growth rates of real GDP, per capita GDP and population**

| **Major Indicators** | | **Constant Price of ($2005)** | | | | | | **Annual Average** | | |
|---|---|---|---|---|---|---|---|---|---|---|
| | | 1981/ 1982 | 1991/ 1992 | 1996/ 1997 | 2001/ 2002 | 2006/ 2007 | 2011/ 2012 | 1982- 1991 | 1992- 2001 | 2002- 2012 |
| Real GDP in ($Billions) | Ethiopia | 5.664 | 5.765 | 8.282 | 9.806 | 15.05 | 23.21 | 6.182 | 7.745 | 15.49 |
| | SSA | 350.1 | 411.9 | 475.8 | 553.9 | 742.6 | 907.5 | 397.0 | 465.5 | 771.6 |
| Real GDP per capita(millions) | Ethiopia | 152.6 | 111.9 | 136.7 | 140.2 | 187.1 | 253.1 | 144.2 | 129.1 | 188.9 |
| | SSA | 870.2 | 768.5 | 775.8 | 791.1 | 930.2 | 994.9 | 823.2 | 766.5 | 974.1 |
| **Indicator** | | **Annual Growth (%)** | | | | | | **Annual Average** | | |
| Real GDP growth | Ethiopia | 0.9 | -8.7 | 3.1 | 1.5 | 11.5 | 8.5 | 1.4 | 4.5 | 8.4 |
| | SSA | 0.6 | -0.9 | 3.7 | 3.5 | 7.0 | 4.2 | 1.7 | 2.6 | 5.2 |
| Real GDP per capita growth | Ethiopia | -1.8 | -11.8 | 0.1 | -1.4 | 8.5 | 5.7 | -1.8 | 1.3 | 5.5 |
| | SSA | -2.2 | -3.6 | 0.9 | 0.8 | 4.2 | 1.5 | -1.1 | -0.1 | 2.2 |

**Source: Own computation based on the data from World Bank, WDI, 2014**

Despite the history of growth performance of Ethiopia was poor in the past, the country has experienced strong economic growth in the current time especially since 2003/04 (Figure 1).

**Figure 1: Ethiopian and Sub-Sahara African GDP annual growth**

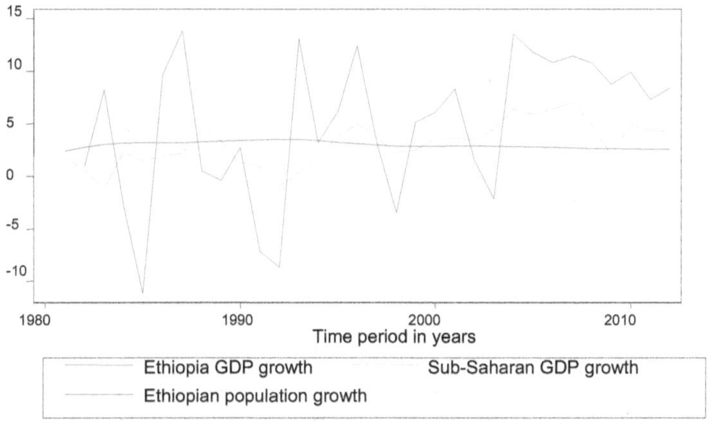


**Source: World Bank World Development Indicator, 2014**

Furthermore, the country has registered a significant upward growth of real GDP per capita from 111.9 to 253.1 $ million from 1991/92-2011/12 with an annual average growth from 129.1 to 188.9 $million in the post Derg regime and then shows a slight decline during the military period. The growth rate of real GDP per capita of country was increased from an annual average of 1.3 to 5.5 percent and the growth records of real GDP per capita growth of Ethiopia was moderately better that that of SSA counties annual average growth rates for the period of 1981/82 to 2011/12. The Ethiopian population growth rate shows more or less steady growth for the period of 1981-2012 (see also figure 1).

### 3.1.2. Sector Wise Analysis of Economic Growth in Ethiopia

Ethiopian economy is grouped under three industrial classifications. These include agriculture, industry and the service sectors. Agriculture plays an important role in terms of employment and its contribution to GDP of Ethiopia. Ethiopian economy is a subsistence economy that is highly dependent on agriculture which in turn depends on vagaries of nature. Over 80 percent of the population depends on agricultural sector for earning as their means of their livelihood.

Agriculture accounts for almost more than half of the GDP and more than 90 percent of the export earnings of the country.

**Figure 2: Share of major industrial sectors value added (% of GDP)**

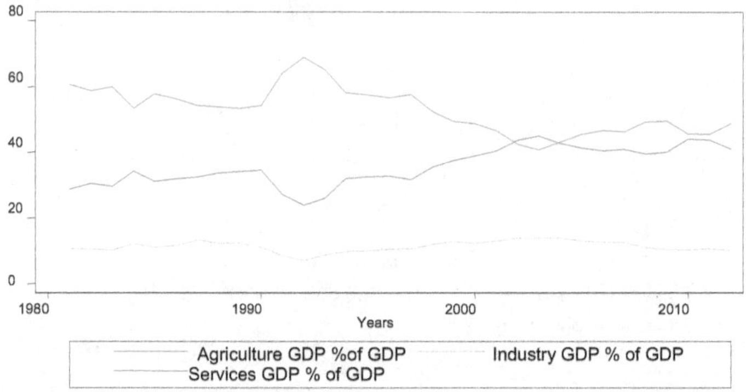


**Source: Own computation based on the data from WB, World Development Indicator, 2014**

Despite agriculture remained the mainstay of the economy of the country, the share of agriculture value added is steadily declining and the declining rate is higher in the recent years around 2002/03 during severe drought shock in the country. In history of more than 30 years, the service sector becomes the dominant sector over agriculture and falls back to its position then after (figure 4). Moreover, its share in total GDP was declined to 48.8 per cent in 2011/12 down from 68.9 per cent of GDP in 1991/1992 in the then government. In 2002/03, the country was under wide spread drought that led to food insecurity for over more than 14 million persons (USAID, 2003).

The agricultural sector accounts for annual average share of GDP of 56.1percent and 45.8 percent of the country between 1990/91-2000/01 and 2001/02-2011/12 respectively. The annual average growth of agriculture during this period was 3.2 percent and 6.1 percent respectively. As the country's economy is highly dependent on agriculture, it is worth mentioning in this regard that much of the fluctuations in real GDP growth rate have been due to variation in rainfall and climatic condition that affects agricultural production as the economy is highly dependent on agriculture. Table 2 summarizes major industrial sectors share of GDP and their annual growth rates.

**Table 2: Annual growth of industrial sectors' value added (% of GDP)**

| Major Indicators | Share of GDP (%) | | | | | | Annual Average | | |
|---|---|---|---|---|---|---|---|---|---|
| | 1981/ 1982 | 1991/ 1992 | 1996/ 1997 | 2001/ 2002 | 2006/ 2007 | 2011/ 2012 | 1982- 1991 | 1992- 2001 | 2002- 2012 |
| Agriculture, value added | 58.8 | 68.9 | 57.6 | 42.5 | 46.4 | 48.8 | 56.6 | 56.1 | 45.8 |
| Industry, value added | 10.7 | 7.2 | 10.7 | 13.9 | 12.6 | 10.1 | 11.4 | 10.7 | 12.1 |
| Service, value added | 30.5 | 23.9 | 31.7 | 43.6 | 41.0 | 41.1 | 32.0 | 33.2 | 42.1 |
| **Growth Indicators** | **Annual Growth (%)** | | | | | | **Annual Average** | | |
| Agriculture, value added | -3.1 | -1.6 | 2.0 | -1.9 | 9.4 | 4.9 | 1.9 | 3.2 | 6.1 |
| Industry, value added | 8.9 | -19.9 | 3.7 | 8.3 | 9.5 | 12.5 | 1.1 | 5.2 | 10.9 |
| Service, value added | 6.6 | -16.3 | 4.3 | 5.5 | 15.7 | 11.3 | 2.1 | 6.6 | 10.7 |
| 1. Education | 16.1 | 18.7 | 11.2 | 7.7 | 21.2 | 4.7 | 8.3 | 14.2 | 11.5 |
| 2. Health | 6.6 | 18.7 | 8.1 | -0.1 | 15.8 | 12.4 | 5.3 | 12 | 11.1 |

**Source: Own computation based on the data from WB, World Development Indicator, 2014**

The industry sector of Ethiopian economy is another sub-sector that shows more or less stable type of economic growth. The share of industry sector accounted for 10.1 per cent of GDP in 2011/12, up from 7.2 percent of GDP of the year 1991/92. The growth performance of the industry sector also rose in 2011/12 to 12.5 percent from 3.7 per cent in 1996/97. The improved industry sector performance was, however, largely as a result of the improved agricultural production that increased the availability of raw materials especially for food processing industries.

The service sector of the economy, that includes education and health sector, refer to economic output of intangible commodities that may be produced, transferred, and consumed at the same time. The share of the services sector that accounted for 23.9 per cent of GDP in 1991/92 is increased to 41.1 per cent in 2011/12. The growth of the services sector also increased to 11.3 per cent in 2011/12 from declining growth rate of 4.3 percent of the year 1996/97. The main growth engine in the services economy during current regime was social services, especially education and health as the government diverted increased resources (including ODA) to these activities. Education service expanded to 21.2 percent annual growth in 2006/07, up from 18.7 percent in 1991/92, while the health sector shows a fluctuating rate of growth since 1991/92.

### 3.1.3. Trends of Domestic Savings and Investment in Ethiopia

Capital formation is regarded as one of the requirements for accelerating economic growth. It is financed by different sources with the main source being domestic savings. In case there is a saving-investment gap, external sources of finance such as loan, aid and foreign direct investment (FDI) can help to bridge the gap. In Ethiopia domestic saving has been well below the required amount to finance the capital formation of the country. The gross capital formation (GCF) of the Derg regime (before 1990/91) was far below the level during the post-1991/92 period due to inappropriate economic policy that it followed. During that period, ownership of means of production was mainly restricted to the government and the role of the private sector in the economy was deliberately reduced to the extent of setting capital ceiling law.

Moreover, foreign direct investment (FDI) as a percentage of GDP was very negligible and the data was in extent for the Derg regime due to the prevailing political turmoil during that period. In the post 1991, due to the change in economic policy and the priority given to the private sector, GCF as a percentage of GDP has been increasing from 10.7 percent of 1991/92 and reached the maximum level of 34.6 percent during 2011/122. For the last three decades, ten years annual average percentage share of GCF to GDP shows increasing trends from 15.1 percent annual average share of GCF to GDP between 1981/82- 1990/91 to 27.4 percentage shares in the present regime during the period of 2001/02-2011/1.

There is no any private capital formation for the Derg regime because of its political and policy condition. But the percentage share of the private sector fixed capital formation (FCF) to GDP was increased from 8.4 percent in 1981/82 to 21.9 percent in 2011/12 in the post Derg period. Annual average private FCF to GDP for the period under consideration was also shows an increasing. It was increased from 5.5 percent of the 19981/82-1990/91 to 13.1 percent annual increments between 2001/02-2011/12. The annual average growth during the above time period was 3.1 percent between 19981/82-1990/91 and reached 39.7 percent in the period between 2001/02-2011/12. The major contributing factor for private sector capital formation growth was the prevailing conducive policy environment of during the post Derg period in Ethiopia. Table 3 summarizes domestic saving, capital formation and FDI inflow.

**Table 3: Domestic saving and capital formation annual growth (% of GDP)**

| Major Indicators | Share of GDP (in %) | | | | | | Annual Average | | |
|---|---|---|---|---|---|---|---|---|---|
| | 1981/ 1982 | 1991/ 1992 | 1996/ 1997 | 2001/ 2002 | 2006/ 2007 | 2011/ 2012 | 1982- 1991 | 1992- 2001 | 2002- 2012 |
| Domestic saving | 9.1 | 6.3 | 13.2 | 13.2 | 4.9 | 16.4 | 10.0 | 10.5 | 9.2 |
| Gross capital formation | 14.7 | 10.7 | 19.8 | 27.3 | 24.4 | 34.6 | 15.1 | 18.9 | 27.4 |
| Private sector FCF | - | 8.4 | 7.8 | 14.9 | 10.4 | 21.9 | 5.5 | 11.0 | 13.1 |
| FDI, net inflows | - | - | 3.2 | 3.3 | 1.2 | 0.7 | - | 1.7 | 2.4 |
| **Growth Indicators** | **Annual Growth (in %)** | | | | | | **Annual Average** | | |
| Domestic saving | -6.0 | -17.5 | 44.8 | -1.0 | 24.9 | 77.9 | 9.8 | 5.1 | 25.3 |
| Gross capital formation | 2.2 | -13.2 | -17.4 | 13.0 | -2.4 | 34.3 | 3.7 | 14.2 | 12.5 |
| Private sector FCF | - | 11.3 | -25.1 | 1.7 | 13.6 | 43.6 | 3.1 | 20.5 | 39.7 |

**Source: Own computation based on the data from WB, World Development Indicator, 2014**

Despite the percentage share of domestic saving to GDP of the country is increasing up to 16.4 percent in the fiscal year 2011/12 from 9.1 percent of the year 1981/82, it could not be able to finance or cover the investment gross capital formation. Provided that the FDI flow into the country has been negligible, the saving-investment gap in Ethiopia implies the importance of foreign finance, mainly aid and loan to fill the gap. Foreign aid is also assumed to facilitate and accelerate the process of development by generating additional domestic savings as a result of the higher growth rates that it is presumed to induce.

### 3.1.4. Trends of External Sector Economic Growth in Ethiopia

In the globalized world where all economies are interlinked in production and exchange of commodities, international trade plays an important role to step forward an economy of a given country. International trade includes export and import of goods and services of a given country. Exports of goods and services represent the value of all goods and other market services provided to the rest of the world. They include the value of merchandise, freight, insurance, transport, travel, royalties, license fees, and other services. Favorable exchange rate policies and improved infrastructure encouraged export performance of a given country in external trade activity. Table 4 summaries the performance of external economic sector of the country for the period of 1981/82 to 2011/12.

**Table 4: Annual growth rate of import and export (% of GDP)**

| Indicators (values of exports & imports) | Value at constant price ($2005) in million | | | | | | Annual average | | |
|---|---|---|---|---|---|---|---|---|---|
| | 1981/ 1982 | 1991/ 1992 | 1996/ 1997 | 2001/ 2002 | 2006/ 2007 | 2011/ 2012 | 1982- 1991 | 19922 001 | 2002- 2012 |
| Exports of goods &S | 388.9 | 187.1 | 992.0 | 1,249 | 1,935 | 3,252 | 383.8 | 784.2 | 2,126 |
| Import of G& service | 707.9 | 443.6 | 1,559 | 2,635 | 4,874 | 7,471 | 702.4 | 1,464 | 4,963 |
| Trade balance (X-M) | -319 | -256.5 | -567 | -1386 | -2939 | -4219 | -318.6 | -679.8 | -2837 |
| **Indicators** | **Share of GDP (%)** | | | | | | **Annual average** | | |
| Exports of goods & S | 6.8 | 3.2 | 11.4 | 12.7 | 12.9 | 14.0 | 6.2 | 9.5 | 13.7 |
| Import of G & service | 12.4 | 7.6 | 17.9 | 26.9 | 32.4 | 32.2 | 11.3 | 17.9 | 31.8 |
| | **Annual growth (%)** | | | | | | **Annual average** | | |
| Exports of goods | -4.1 | -6.5 | 11.2 | 4.8 | 4.0 | 2.5 | 2.7 | 3.6 | 9.2 |
| Import of G& service | 4.7 | -24.2 | 18.3 | 14.0 | -2.4 | 8.7 | -0.5 | 18.6 | 11.8 |

**Source: Own computation based on the data from WB, World Development Indicator, 2014**

Ethiopian export of goods and services shows significant annual average growth in post Derg regime than the period before. The value of export of goods and services of the country at a constant price of 2005$ shows an increasing trend in the two regime in Ethiopia. It was increased up from 388.9 million US$ of 1981/82 fiscal year to 3,252 million in the year 2011/12. An annual average of the value of export of goods and services was also increased to 2,126 million between 2001/02-2011/12 up from 383.8 million between 1981//82-1990/91. But, this value does no show whether this increment is a real increment of the economy. Therefore, it is better to look in terms of GDP of the country and its growth rate.

The total percentage share of export to GDP of the country has grown up to 14 percent in the year 2011/12 from 3.2 percent of the year 1991/92. The ten years annual average share of export to GDP was also increased from 6.2 percent in 1981/2-1990/92 to 13.7 percent for the period between 2001/01-2011/12. According to MoFED (2011) report, the major export commodity that the country exports during this period was agricultural products such as coffee, pulses, oil seeds, fruit and vegetable, meat (canned and frozen), live animals, and chat. Gold and semi-processed products such as leather and leather products are also major export products the country exports to the rest of the country (MoFED, 2011).

For developing economies like Ethiopia, import of goods and services also plays an important role as it supplies capital goods that could not be produced locally, and it also augments local production through delivering necessary raw materials and intermediate goods (Tofik, 2012). Imports of goods and services comprise all transactions between residents of a country and the rest of the world involving a change of ownership from nonresidents to residents of general merchandise, nonmonetary gold, and services. It is the value of all goods and other market services received from the rest of the world.

The value of imported goods and services was increased up to 7,471 million $USD from 404.6 million $ USD of the 1991/92 fiscal year in the post Derg period. An annual percentage share of import of goods and services to GDP during Derg regime shows a rebounding value of around 11.3percent. However, in the post Derg regime, there are significant increments owing to the demand of capital goods for economic development of the country. According to MoFED (2011) report, the highest value of import was on capital goods followed by consumer goods, raw materials, semi finished products, fuel, and others.

Despite the fact that, the total volume of import bill reached 32.2percent of the country's GDP in 2011/12 up from 12.4 percent of the 1981/82 in the post Derg, it requires enough exports to get the foreign exchange required to finance those imports. However, given the country's heavy dependence on agricultural production, mainly subsistence which is backward in nature, it was not able to generate enough revenue from exporting enough commodities and has been suffering from continuous trade deficits. For this reason the trade balance of the country shows increasing trends from time to time as shown by figure 3.

**Figure 3: Export, import, and trade balance trends (% of GDP)**

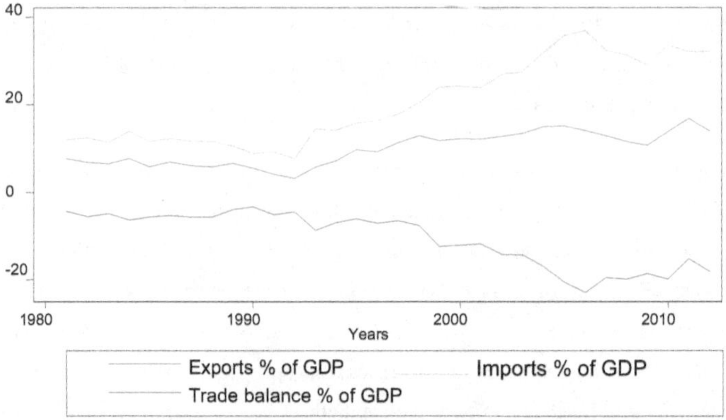


**Source: Own computation based on the data from WB, World Development Indicator, 2014**

The result of the study shows that during period under review, the country has been facing a trade deficit, which has been getting wider and wider reaching almost USD 4.2 billion in 2011/12 from 319 million USD of 1981/82. Similarly, the ten year annual average of trade balance was also increased up to 2,837 million USD for the period of 2001/02-2011/12 from 319 million of the fiscal year between 1981/82-1991/92 (table 4 and figure 3). The reason is that Ethiopia remained to be exporter of agricultural commodities, which has income inelastic demand and a have very volatile price in the international market. On the opposite side, country's imports are manufactured goods, which are highly valuable and costly commodity to cover its value by the revenue generated from bulky and cheap agricultural products.

With respect to the financing of trade deficit of Ethiopia, official development assistance remained to be the most important for the country. The deficit has also made the country to become over-indebted as the remaining part of deficit has also been financed through foreign borrowing. External finance (both loans and grants) can play a critical role in supplementing domestic resources in order to relieve savings or foreign exchange bottlenecks.

### 3.1.5. Government Expenditure and Economic Growth

One way of analyzing the relationship between total government expenditure and real GDP is by looking at the trend of the two together on the same coordinate plane. Direct correlation between government expenditure and real GDP implies there is a positive relationship between the two variables which was in line with Keynesian explanation of the role of government spending in stimulating an economy which is below full employment (Tofik, 2012). However, looking at the gross figures does of total expenditure does not show the size of government commitment relative to the economy. Thus, it is necessary to scrutinize the trend of government expenditure as a percentage of GDP, which can clearly depict the size of the government in the economy.

During the Derg regime, the ratio of government expenditure to GDP had shown a steady growth as a consequence of its socialist policy measures. By then the government was engaged in the production and distribution of private goods and services, which could otherwise be provided by the private sector. During the Derg regime, annual average percentage of public spending to GDP had shows a slight increase to 9.7 percent in 1986/87-1990/91 up from 4.6 percent of 1977/78-1980/81. The growth during this period was driven by expenditure by general services of which internal order and justice and national defense takes the lion's share of expenditure. Moreover, the share of capital expenditure is far below that of current expenditure due to the limited revenue source of the government as the private sector involvement in the economy (figure 4).

However due to the reform in expenditure policy in 1991, capital expenditure kept on growing while current expenditure has been decreasing continuously. An annual average share of capital expenditure to GDP was increased to 24.6 percent between 2006/07-2010/11 up from an annual average of 2.9 percent between 1991/92-1995/96. Annual average shares of capital expenditure to GDP in the past five years were higher than the corresponding current expenditure of the period in nominal terms. The increase in capital expenditure was driven at first by higher economic development spending followed by social development in which agriculture, education and health sector takes the lions share during the post Derg period. The share of capital expenditure to total expenditure shows an increasing trends in the post Derg period as compared to the corresponding current expenditure of the period. It was increased to 54 percent between 2006/07-2010/11 up from 35 percent of an annual average share of capital expenditure to total expenditure between 1991/92-1995/96.

**Figure 4: Current & Capital expenditure, Revenue, & Grant (% of GDP)**

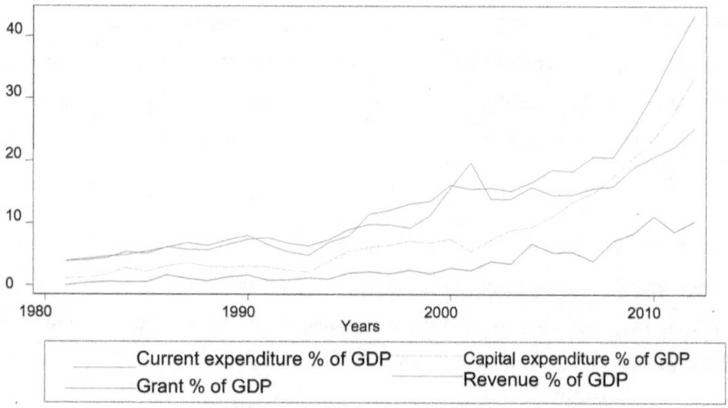


**Source: Own computation on the basis of data from MoFED**

Furthermore, the ratio of capital expenditure to total expenditure has more than doubled (54%) during 2006/07-2010/11 compared to the level (22.8%) during 1977/78-1980/81. It is worth mentioning in this regard that during these periods the country has registered an average growth rate of more than 10 percent. Thus, the result reveals that government's effort to divert its expenditures towards building the capacity of the country in the production of goods and provision of economic and social services during the post-1991 period had helped the country to grow significantly.

The flow of ODA to Ethiopia was very low during the Derg regime due to the policy issues and political turmoil prevailed in the country. The share of ODA to GDP in the Derg period was half percent between 1977/78-1980/81 and was grown to 11.6 percent between 1986/87-1990/91. The reform period has attracted a sizeable increase of external assistance. The share of

ODA to GDP was better in the post period showing an increment from 1.7 percent between 1991/92-1995/96 to 9.2 percent between 2006/07-2010/11 (Table 5).

**Table 5: Current, capital, & external assistance share of GDP and total expenditure**

| Expenditure Category | Share of GDP during Derg | | | Share of GDP in Post Derg | | | |
|---|---|---|---|---|---|---|---|
| | 1977/78 - 1980/81 | 1981/82 - 1985/86 | 1986/87 - 1990/91 | 1991/92 - 1995/96 | 1996/97 - 2000/01 | 2001/02 - 2005/06 | 2006/07 - 2010/11 |
| Current expenditure | 3.6 | 5.4 | 6.8 | 8.5 | 14.0 | 15.0 | 20.6 |
| Capital expenditure | 1.0 | 2.7 | 2.9 | 4.8 | 6.9 | 11.5 | 24.6 |
| Total expenditure | 4.6 | 8.1 | 9.7 | 13.3 | 20.9 | 26.5 | 45.3 |
| External assistance | 0.5 | 0.9 | 11.6 | 1.7 | 2.7 | 5.0 | 9.2 |
| | Share of Total Expenditure (%) | | | | | | |
| Current expenditure | 77.8 | 67.1 | 70.2 | 65.0 | 66.0 | 56.8 | 46 |
| Capital expenditure | 22.8 | 32.9 | 28.8 | 35.0 | 34.0 | 43.2 | 54 |
| Total expenditure | 10.0 | 100.0 | 100.0 | 100.0 | 100.0 | 100.0 | 100 |
| External assistance | 8.3 | 10.4 | 16.5 | 12.0 | 12.5 | 17.3 | 20.5 |

**Source: Own computation based on the data obtained from MoFED**

The growth effect of government expenditure can be analyzed by categorizing it into three as expenditure on investment, consumption and human capital. In doing so, government total capital expenditure less capital expenditure on health and education is considered as investment expenditure. Government total current expenditure less current expenditure on health and education is considered to be expenditure on consumption. The sum of capital and current expenditure on health and education makes up for government expenditure on human capital (Ram, 1986). This is because the physical and mental health of the citizen is very crucial for human capital development and productivity. Thus, the study is an evident that Ethiopia is on the right truck of investing its resources in human capital development.

### 3.1.6. Foreign Aid (ODA) and Economic Growth in Ethiopia

Foreign capital inflows are receiving due attention because of their potential to finance investment and perceived to promote economic growth in the recipient country. The growing divergence in saving and investment rates, export-import gap (foreign exchange constraints to import capital goods) and budget deficits in Ethiopia make to depend highly on inflow of foreign capital. Aid can finance investment directly by filling the savings-investment gap and can indirectly fill the foreign exchange gap. As official aid is issued to government, it can also fund government spending and compensate for a small domestic tax base. The capability of Ethiopia in improving the level of investment and promotion of economic growth through domestic capital sources (revenue generation) and private capital inflow alone is far from adequate to finance government spending demand. This makes the importance of foreign aid indisputable to the performance of the economy in addition to domestically generated revenue.

Foreign aid plays an important role in the economic development programs of successive Ethiopian governments since 1960. It consists of loans and grants by official agencies of the members of the DAC, multilateral institutions, and by non-DAC countries to promote economic development and welfare in countries and territories in the DAC list of ODA recipients. During the Derg regime, the average grant element has declined tremendously and stood at 39 percent in1986/87-1990/91 from 54.5 percent of 1977/78-1980/81 implying that the share of the loan element has increasing while the grant element was decreasing. However, the grant element shows an increasing trend in the post Derg period and become reached an average grant element of 61.4 percent in 2006/07-2011/12.

During the period 1977/78-1990/91, net ODA shows stagnation with an annual average of 5.3 percent of GNI in Ethiopia. However, it was increased to 12.2 percent in 2011/12 up from 7.6 percent annual average of 1986/87 of the Derg regime. An annual average percentage share of net ODA to GDP of the country also shows similar trends with that of per capita ODA in the past two regimes (Table 6).

**Table 6: Percentage shares of net ODA to economic sectors**

| Major Indicator | Derg period | | | EPRDF (Post Derg) | | | |
|---|---|---|---|---|---|---|---|
| | 1977/78 - 1980/81 | 1981/82 - 1985/86 | 1986/87 - 1990/91 | 1991/92 - 1995/96 | 1996/97 - 2000/01 | 2001/02 - 2005/06 | 2006/07 - 2011/12 |
| Average grant element (%) | 54.5 | 46.2 | 39.0 | 73.5 | 74.4 | 60.4 | 61.4 |
| Net ODA (% of GNI) | 3.4 | 5.0 | 7.6 | 12.1 | 9.1 | 16.9 | 12.2 |
| Net ODA (% of GCF) | 23.2 | 35.7 | 52.1 | 79.1 | 40.3 | 62.0 | 45.8 |
| Net ODA per capita | 5.2 | 11.2 | 18.9 | 18.3 | 11.4 | 23.5 | 38.8 |
| Net ODA (% of GDP) | 3.4 | 5.0 | 7.6 | 12.0 | 9.0 | 16.8 | 12.2 |

**Source: Own computation based on the data from World Bank WDI, 2104**

The annual percentage share of net ODA to gross capital formation (GCF) of Ethiopia during the Derg regime was increased to 52.1 percent in the year 1986/87-1990/91 up from 23.2 percent of its average share between 1977/78/-1980/81. However, the annual average share of net ODA to GCF decline from 79.1 percent of 1991/92-1995/96 to 45.8 percent in the year between 2005/06-2011/12 in the post-Derg regime. The main reason for the decline in annual average share of net ODA to GCF in the recent period was not due to the decline in the flow of foreign aid but due to an increasing trend in GCF of the country from 2005/06- 2011/12.

### 3.1.7. Sectoral Composition of Foreign Aid (ODA) in Ethiopia

Official development assistance is a commonly used measure of developmental aid. Development aid is given by governments through individual countries' international aid agencies, multilateral institutions, and by individuals through development charities that includes programme aid that is given for a specific sector. Source wise data depict that aid from multilateral sources has increased gradually whereas aid from bilateral sources has decreasing since 1960. Despite bilateral aid shows declining trends, it is greater than that of multilateral aid for the last fifty years. The share of non DAC flow of ODA to Ethiopia was insignificant (Figure 5).

**Figure 5: Flow of Bilateral, multilateral and Non DAC aid to Ethiopia**

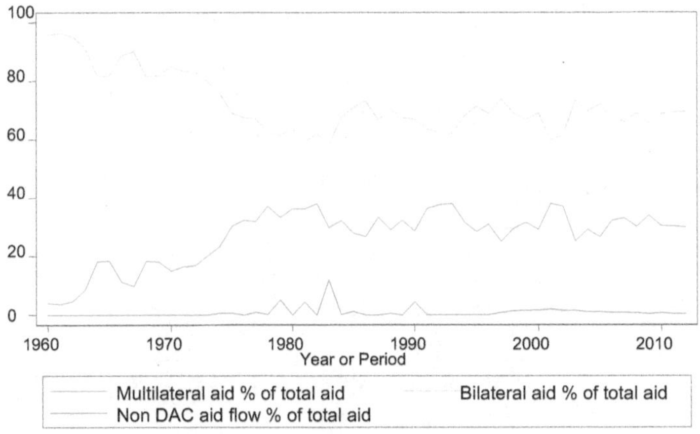


**Source: Own computation based on the data from World Bank WDI, 2104**

Analysis of aid flows to sectors with recipient's country wise in the context of the total aid flow during the past three or more decades is greatly hampered by the lack of complete, reliable, and consistent data. The only systematic data available for aid flows over time have been compiled by the OECD/DAC. However, the easily accessible OECD/DAC website does not provide a consistent and comparable breakdown of aid flows from both multilateral and bilateral donors from the early 1970s to the present. This source provides a sectoral classification of aid flows from the 1973 onward only for the bilateral aid total to all recipients and not for the rest of the donors. The sectoral classification of the total aid flows to individual country like Ethiopia is available only from 1995 to the present. Moreover, the data that is available regarding aid to the sector from the OCED/DAC database has a category of "multi-sectoral" aid that includes aid to more than one sector. Therefore, it is not known how much aid directly goes to which sector at the destination of the recipient country.

The sectoral distribution of the total aid disbursed to Ethiopia is classified as social infrastructure & services, economic infrastructure & services, production sector, multi-sector or cross cutting issues, programme assistance/ commodity aid, general budget support, action related to debit, humanitarian and others (Tables 7).

**Table 7: Three years average share of sectoral distribution of aid (% of total aid)**

| Major AID sectors | 1994/95 - 1996/97 | 1997/98 - 1999/00 | 2000/01 - 2002/03 | 2003/04 -205/06 | 2006/07 - 2008/09 | 2009/10 - 2011/12 |
|---|---|---|---|---|---|---|
| Social infrastructure & services | 24.3 | 35.1 | 29.9 | 32.6 | 45.4 | 30.5 |
| Education | 4.9 | 7.7 | 6.0 | 6.6 | 5.6 | 6.1 |
| Health | 4.8 | 6.7 | 4.9 | 5.3 | 7.4 | 7.4 |
| Economic infrastructure & services | 20.7 | 21.9 | 13.1 | 20.2 | 13.6 | 18.8 |
| Production sector | 20.7 | 7.5 | 12.5 | 4.4 | 7.0 | 9.1 |
| Agriculture | 18.2 | 6.5 | 6.3 | 2.7 | 6.1 | 6.7 |
| Multi-sector/crosscutting | 4.9 | 2.1 | 2.7 | 5.0 | 10.1 | 10.1 |
| Program assistance/commodity aid | 13.7 | 20.0 | 16.1 | 12.1 | 7.2 | 11.1 |
| General budget support | 4.3 | 2.6 | 6.8 | 6.0 | 1.3 | 4.0 |
| Action related to debt | 9.5 | 1.4 | 3.3 | 7.6 | 0.4 | 0.1 |
| Humanitarian aid | 5.2 | 11.0 | 21.3 | 17.3 | 16.1 | 15.3 |
| Administrative & others total | 0.8 | 1.1 | 1.1 | 0.7 | 0.3 | 0.4 |
| Total all sectors | 100 | 100 | 100 | 100 | 100 | 100 |

**Source: Own computation from OECD- DAC/CRS data base**

Social infrastructure and services has accounted for the largest share in the total aid. Its share has increased over time to 45.4 percent in 2006/07-2008/09 up from 24.3 percent share in 1994/95-1996/97 and then started to decline to share of 30.5percent in the period between 2009/10-2011/12. The health and education components of the social infrastructure and services had consistently large shares in the total aid. The share of both health and education together was 9.7 percent of the total aid in 1994/95-1996/97, increasing to about 13.5 percent in 2009/10-2011/12, with the share of aid to education being consistently higher from 1994/95-2005/06 than that of health and the health sector become higher thereafter.

Furthermore, the share of the production sector, meaning agriculture, industry and mining, and trade policies and tourism in the total aid was 12.3 percent in 1994/95-1996/97, dropping to 9.1 percent in 2009/10- 2011/12. The share of aid to agriculture in total aid decreased from 18.2 percent in 1994/95-1996/97 to about 2.7 percent in 2003/04-2005/06, and it then increased to 6.7 percent in 2009/10-2011/12.

The share of economic infrastructure and services throughout was lower than that of social infrastructure and services, the former's share in total aid decreased from 20.7 percent in 1994/95-1996/97 to 18.8 percent in 2009/10-2011/12. Multi-sector/crosscutting aid started from a very insignificant base and started to increase its share during the 1990s. Its share in the total aid varied between 2.1 and 10.1 percent since 1994/95. The increase in multi-sector aid from 2003/04 onwards was partly due to an increasing emphasis on interdependence among sectors and the synergistic effects of development in one sector on the other.

The corresponding figures for commodity aid or general programme assistance shows an increment in the 1990s and then it starts to decline from the maximum share of 20 percent in 19997/98-1999/00 to 7.2 percent in 2006/07-2008/09 and then it starts to increase to 11.1 percent in the period between 2009/10-2011/12. General budget support, which was relatively unimportant component of program assistance, varies between 1.3 to 6.8 percent in the total aid. During the period of 2000/01-2002/03, it was reached a maximum of 6.8 percent and subsequently declined to about 1.3 percent in 2006/07-2008/09 and then started to increase to 4 percent 2009/10-2011/12. Under this form of aid, resources are placed at the disposal of governments to meet the overall deficiency of revenue resources, without earmarking the aid for any sector. Instead, it is left up to recipient governments to allocate among sectors and purposes of aid, with some broad objectives usually agreed upon by the donors and the recipient governments. Thus, it is not possible to allocate such aid to any one sector.

## 3.2. Empirical Results Analysis and Interpretations

### 3.2.1. Results for Unit-Root Test

Non stationarity of time series data has often been regarded as a problem in empirical analysis. To apply the correct methodology as well as time to avoid any spurious inferences from a given regression, it is necessary to investigate whether the data series is stationary in level, or stationary in differences. Testing stationary of time series leads to the implementation of the econometric model by employing the Augmented Dickey-Fuller (ADF) unit root test. Since unit root tests are sensitive to the presence of deterministic regressors, the three models are estimated.

For this study, the most general model with a drift and time trend is estimated first and restrictive models i.e. with a constant and without either constant and trend, respectively, are estimated. Unit root tests for each variable, is performed on both levels and first differences. The ADF test results show that most the variables (in levels) are non stationary (contain a unit root) with the three different specifications. Furthermore, the first differences of the variables are investigated for a unit root and the test result proved that most of the variables are stationary at their I(1). Table 8 summarizes the ADF test result of the growth equation.

The test result in table 8 reveals that some of the variables in growth equation are stationary at level. Such variables include real GDP, government expenditure (GOV), total foreign aid (FAID) and domestic savings of the country (SAV) are stationary at their respective level, I(0), if no trend are included. Foreign aid allocated to agricultural sector (AGRIAID), educational sector (EDUCAID), health sector (HEALAID), agricultural sector GDP (AGDP), educational sector GDP (EDGDP), health sector GDP (HEGDP) and are stationary at level in the three cases. However, if drift and trend are included, all variables except openness to trade (TRADE) and private capital flow (PRIV) are stationary at level. Openness to trade and net private capital flow become stationary at their first difference (Table 8).

**Table 8: ADF unit root test result for variables in growth equation**

| Variables | | Without cons & trend | | ADF with trend | | With drift & trend | | stationary at |
|---|---|---|---|---|---|---|---|---|
| | | @level | @ I(1) | @level | @ I(1) | @level | @ I(1) | |
| Real GDP | | 8.041** | | 2.891 | | 7.363** | | I(0) |
| FAID | | -0.380 | -4.266** | -1.287 | -4.426** | -1.880* | -4.200** | I(0) |
| GOV | | 6.742** | | 2.331 | | 4.713** | | I(0) |
| SAV | | -0.516 | -7.822** | -2.959 | -7.679** | -3.084* | -7.722** | I(0) |
| EDUCAID | | -2.211* | | -7.068** | | -6.834** | | I(0) |
| HEALAID | | -2.710** | | -6.313** | | -5.557** | | I(0) |
| AGRIAID | | -1.593* | | -4.346** | | -4.415** | | I(0) |
| AGDP | | 9.109** | | 6.268** | | 8.738** | | I(0) |
| EDGDP | | 19.543** | | 8.290** | | 15.503** | | I(0) |
| HGDP | | 12.243** | | 9.738** | | 11.734** | | I(0) |
| dPRIV | | 0.474 | -4.989** | -2.032 | -5.188** | -1.208 | -5.239** | I(1) |
| dTRADE | | 1.090 | -4.816** | -2.066 | -4.946** | -0.434 | -5.034** | I(1) |
| Critical Value | 1% | -2.650 | -2.652 | -4.325 | -4.334 | -2.462 | -2.467 | |
| | 5% | -1.950 | -1.950 | -3.576 | -3.580 | -1.699 | -1.701 | |

**Note: d represents the first difference of the time series variable, ** and * represent variables are significant at 1 percent and 5 percent Mackinnon critical values for rejection of hypothesis of a unit root respectively. d implies first differencing of the variables.**

Since unit root tests often suffer from poor size and power property, (i.e., the tendency to over-reject the null hypothesis of non stationary when it is true and under reject the null when it is false, respectively) it is quite common to proceed to tests for co-integration even when the unit root tests suggest that the variables are unbalanced. In other words, it is possible that co-integration is present even when there is a mix of I(0) and I(1) variables in the model (Harris, 1995; Martins, 2010). Hence, the above unit root tests result do not prohibit one to employ the Johanson Maximum Likelihood Procedure to test for the existence of co-integration.

### 3.2.2. Co-integration and Long run Growth Equation Analysis

The implication that non-stationary variables can lead to spurious regressions unless there is at least one co-integration vector is that some form of testing for co-integration is almost mandatory. For this study, co-integration tests methodology developed by Johanson is applied.

In Johanson procedure, the likelihood ratio (LR) test is used to test the significance of estimates of $\lambda_i$ eigenvalues. $\lambda_{race}$ and $\lambda_{max}$ statistics are used to test the number of characteristic roots that are insignificantly different from unity. The trace statistics tests whether there is at most one co-integrating relationship while the maximal statistics used to test the null hypothesis that there are r co-integrating vectors as against the alternative hypothesis of r<1. To determine the number of co-integrating relations r, we can proceed sequentially from r = 0 to r = n-1 until we fail to reject the hypothesis.

The diagnostic tests show that the model has passed all tests. The result of the study shows that the null of no co-integration is rejected at 1percent and 5 percent level of significance while the alternative hypothesis that at least one co-integrating vector is not rejected by λtrace statistics. This suggests that there exist precisely one co-integrating vector in the estimated model. Hence, we can conclude that there is one long-run relationship between the variables which is explained by a linear combination of I(0) and I(1) variables at an aggregate notional level (Table 9).

**Table 9: Johansen co-integration tests result for aggregate Ethiopian economy**

| Ho: (null Hyp) | Ha | Eigenvalue ($\lambda_i$) | λmax Statistic | critical value | | λtrace Statistic | critical value | |
|---|---|---|---|---|---|---|---|---|
| | | | | 5% | 1% | | 5% | 1% |
| r= 0 | r=1 | 0.78043 | 43.9660 | 40.30 | 45.10 | 128.3788* | 102.14 | 103.18 |
| r≤1 | R=2 | 0.68252 | 33.2732 | 34.40 | 38.77 | 84.4128* | 76.07 | 76.07 |
| r≤ 2 | r=3 | 0.54671 | 22.9456 | 28.14 | 32.24 | 51.1396 | 53.12 | 54.46 |
| r≤ 3 | r=4 | 0.40723 | 15.1653 | 22.00 | 25.52 | 28.1940 | 34.91 | 35.65 |
| r ≤4 | r=5 | 0.25837 | 8.6683 | 15.67 | 18.63 | 13.0287 | 19.96 | 20.04 |
| r≤ 5 | r=6 | 0.13960 | 4.3604 | 9.24 | 6.65 | 4.3604 | 9.42 | 6.65 |
| Vector AR-2 F (6, 25) = 6.7111[0.0000] and number of lags used=2. | | | | | | | | |

**Note: r denotes the number of co-integrating vectors * denotes rejection of the null at 1percent and 5percent significance level. Variables entered unrestricted are constant.**

Similarly, the result of co-integration test for agriculture, education and health sector was described as by the table 10-12 specified bellow. The result of sectoral analysis of variables reveals that the null of no co-integration is rejected at 1percent and 5percent level of significance while the alternative hypothesis that at least one co-integrating vector is not rejected by λtrace statistics. This suggests that there exist precisely one co-integrating vector in the estimated model.

**Table 10: Johansen co-integration tests result for agricultural sector**

| Ho: (null hypothesis) | Ha | Eigen value ($\lambda_i$) | λmax Statistic | critical value | | λtrace Statistic | critical value | |
|---|---|---|---|---|---|---|---|---|
| | | | | 5% | 1% | | 5% | 1% |
| r= 0 | r=1 | 0.77729 | 43.5550 | 39.37 | 45.10 | 118.9830* | 94.15 | 103.18 |
| r≤1 | r=2 | 0.62855 | 28.7203 | 33.46 | 38.77 | 75.4280 | 68.52 | 76.07 |
| r≤ 2 | r=3 | 0.56975 | 24.4583 | 27.07 | 32.24 | 46.7078 | 47.21 | 54.46 |
| r≤ 3 | r=4 | 0.38210 | 13.9615 | 20.97 | 25.52 | 22.2495 | 29.68 | 35.65 |
| r ≤4 | r=5 | 0.24416 | 8.1177 | 14.07 | 18.63 | 8.2880 | 15.41 | 20.04 |
| r≤ 5 | r=6 | 0.00585 | 0.1702 | 3.76 | 6.65 | 0.1702 | 3.76 | 6.65 |

**Note: r denotes the number of co-integrating vectors and * denotes rejection of the null at 1 and 5percent significance level**

**Table 11: Johansen co-integration tests result for educational sector**

| Ho: (null hypothesis) | Ha | Eigen value ($\lambda_i$) | λmax Statistic | critical value | | λtrace Statistic | critical value | |
|---|---|---|---|---|---|---|---|---|
| | | | | 5% | 1% | | 5% | 1% |
| r= 0 | r=1 | 0.72998 | 37.9690 | 39.37 | 45.10 | 123.3391 | 94.15 | 103.18 |
| r≤1 | r=2 | 0.69458 | 34.3960 | 33.46 | 38.77 | 85.3701* | 68.52 | 76.07 |
| r≤ 2 | r=3 | 0.64286 | 29.8592 | 27.07 | 32.24 | 50.9741 | 47.21 | 54.46 |
| r≤ 3 | r=4 | 0.38969 | 14.3197 | 20.97 | 25.52 | 21.1149 | 29.68 | 35.65 |
| r ≤4 | r=5 | 0.14221 | 4.4484 | 14.07 | 18.63 | 6.7952 | 15.41 | 20.04 |
| r≤ 5 | r=6 | 0.07774 | 2.3468 | 3.76 | 6.65 | 2.3468 | 3.76 | 6.65 |

**Note: r denotes the number of co-integrating vectors and * denotes rejection of the null at 1 and 5percent significance level**

**Table 12: Johansen co-integration tests for health sector**

| Ho: (null hypothesis) | Ha | Eigen value ($\lambda_i$) | λmax Statistic | critical value | | λtrace Statistic | critical value | |
|---|---|---|---|---|---|---|---|---|
| | | | | 5% | 1% | | 5% | 1% |
| r= 0 | r=1 | 0.73633 | 38.6588 | 39.37 | 45.10 | 105.8687* | 94.15 | 103.18 |
| r≤1 | r=2 | 0.65508 | 30.8689 | 33.46 | 38.77 | 67.2099 | 68.52 | 76.07 |
| r≤ 2 | r=3 | 0.46157 | 17.9540 | 27.07 | 32.24 | 36.3410 | 47.21 | 54.46 |
| r≤ 3 | r=4 | 0.35738 | 12.8239 | 20.97 | 25.52 | 18.3870 | 29.68 | 35.65 |
| r ≤4 | r=5 | 0.17379 | 5.5362 | 14.07 | 18.63 | 5.5630 | 15.41 | 20.04 |
| r≤ 5 | r=6 | 0.00092 | 0.0268 | 3.76 | 6.65 | 0.0268 | 3.76 | 6.65 |

**Note: r denotes the number of co-integrating vectors and * denotes rejection of the null at 1 and 5percent significance level**

Once the existence of co-integrating vector is statistically supported, what is relevant for our analysis is the first column of the α matrix (the matrix of speed of adjustment coefficients) and the first row of the β matrix (long-run coefficients of the variables) in table 13 and 14.

**Table 13: Normalized long run β Coefficients of aggregate & sectoral level**

| Aggregate Real GDP | Real GDP | FAID | dPRIV | dTRADE | SAV | GOV |
|---|---|---|---|---|---|---|
| | 1.000 | -4786.74 | 21408.56 | 4930.177 | 2370.383 | -2605.557 |
| Agricultural GDP | AGDP | agriaid | dPRIV | dTRADE | SAV | GOV |
| | 1.000 | -15572.01 | -12200.23 | -5242.691 | 1674.624 | 260.021 |
| Education GDP | EDGDP | EDUAID | dPRIV | dTRADE | SAV | GOV |
| | 1.000 | -4705.957 | 81.97008 | 271.0293 | -378.8908 | 22.42045 |
| Health sector GD | HGDP | HEALAID | dPRIV | dTRADE | SAV | GOV |
| | 1.000 | -17.04431 | 12.70707 | 17.86084 | -5.621293 | -37.49298 |

**Table 14: Adjustment (α) coefficients of aggregate and sectoral level**

| Aggregate real GDP | | Agriculture sector | | Educational sector | | Health sector | |
|---|---|---|---|---|---|---|---|
| variable | coefficient | variable | coefficient | variable | coefficient | variable | coefficient |
| D_realgdp | -.0714923 | D_agdp | .249695 | D_edgdp | .0629386 | D_hegdp | .6801234 |
| D_faid | -.0000183 | D_agriaid | 1.49e-06 | Deducaid | .0002395 | Dhealaid | .0000453 |
| D_dpriv | -.0000486 | D_dpriv | .0000189 | D_dpriv | -.0003134 | D_dpriv | -.0005875 |
| D_dtrade | -.0001087 | D_dtrade | .00001 | D_dtrade | -.0003111 | D_dtrade | -.0007097 |
| D_sav | .0000264 | D_sav | .0000271 | D_sav | .0007784 | D_sav | .0115856 |
| D_gov | 8.66e-06 | D_gov | .0000131 | D_gov | .0001363 | D_gov | .0069639 |

A well known problem with VARs and particularly important in the identification of a VECM is the prohibitively large number of parameters. Each equation involves estimating $m$ x $k$ lag coefficients plus one or more parameters for the deterministic components, where $m$ and $k$ represents number of variables and number of lags included in the system respectively. One way to address the over-parameterization problem is to test and impose weak exogeneity assumptions (Zhou, Bonham, & Gangnes, 2007).

Thus in order to indentify the variables that are endogenously determined and conditional on the other explanatory variables in the model, a weak exogeneity test is conducted. As a result the likelihood ratio test is made by imposing zero restriction on the relevant α coefficient (first column of α coefficient matrix) given above. This is essentially a test for weak exogeneity which helps to identify endogenous and exogenous variables in the model. Rejection of weak exogeneity implies that the variables under investigation are endogenous.

Table 15 summarizes the result of tests for weak exogeneity. The likelihood ratio test result indicated that except for real GDP, private capital flow and trade, none of the variables reject the null hypothesis that all the variables are weakly exogenous. Therefore real GDP, private capital flow, and trade are endogenously determined in the model while the other explanatory variables are weakly exogenous to the system. Thus it is valid to condition on the weakly exogenous variables. This enables us to analyze a single long run equation for real GDP conditional on the variables which are not endogenously determined in the model.

At the sectoral level, the likelihood ratio test result indicated that except for real agricultural GDP, educational sector GDP, education sector foreign aid, health sector GDP, domestic saving and government expenditure (which are endogenously determined in the model), none of the variables reject the null hypothesis that all the remaining variables are weakly exogenous to the system.

**Table 15: Results of weak exogeneity test for aggregate and sectorial levels**

| **Aggregate** | **D_realgdp** | **D_faid** | **D_dpriv** | **D_dtrade** | **D_sav** | **D_gov** |
|---|---|---|---|---|---|---|
| $\alpha$ | -.0714923 | -.0000183 | -.0000486 | -.0001087 | .0000264 | 8.66e-06 |
| $\chi^2$ | 4.484147 | .6671795 | 11.276 | 9.961305 | .6166376 | .1456655 |
| P-value | 0.0342* | 0.4140 | 0.0008** | 0.0016** | 0.4323 | 0.7027 |
| **Agriculture** | **D_agdp** | **D_agriaid** | **D_dpriv** | **D_dtrade** | **D_sav** | **D_gov** |
| $\alpha$ | .249695 | 1.49e-06 | .0000189 | .00001 | .0000271 | .0000131 |
| $\chi^2$ | 5.477878 | .1423019 | 2.642973 | .1058688 | 1.299999 | .8811752 |
| P-value | 0.0193* | 0.7060 | 0.1040 | 0.7449 | 0.2542 | 0.3479 |
| **Education** | **D_edgdp** | **Deducaid** | **D_dpriv** | **D_dtrade** | **D_sav** | **D_gov** |
| $\alpha$ | .0629386 | .0002395 | -.0003134 | -.0003111 | .0007784 | .0001363 |
| $\chi^2$ | 6.156519 | 16.60161 | 2.0133 | .2946335 | 3.784347 | .3046427 |
| P-value | 0.0131* | 0.0000** | 0.1559 | 0.5873 | 0.0517* | 0.5810 |
| **Health** | **D_hegdp** | **D-healaid** | **D_dpriv** | **D_dtrade** | **D_sav** | **D_gov** |
| $\alpha$ | .6801234 | 0000453 | -.0005875 | -.0007097 | .0115856 | .0069639 |
| $\chi^2$ | 19.53029 | .00123 | .034605 | .0085541 | 5.104146 | 6.82496 |
| P-value | 0.0000** | 0.9720 | 0.8524 | 0.9263 | 0.0239* | 0.0090** |

**Note: ** and * represent rejection of weak exogeneity at1% and 5% level of significance.**

Similarly zero restriction is imposed on long run β coefficients to identify which explanatory variables constituting the growth equation are statistically different from zero. The result of the likelihood ratio test shows that there are also weakly exogenous variables in the system both at aggregate and sectoral level. The zero restriction test performed on the long run coefficients of the explanatory variables shows the statistically significant coefficient different from zero for aggregate and sectoral level for agriculture, education, and health sector, which allows the estimation of the long run growth equation.

**Table 16: Result of zero restriction test on β coefficients for aggregate and sectors**

| Real GDP | **D_faid** | **D_dpriv** | **D_dtrade** | **D_sav** | **D_gov** |
|---|---|---|---|---|---|
| Coefficient-β | -4786.7k4 | 21408.56 | 4930.177 | 2370.383 | -2605.557 |
| $\chi^2$ | 8.137878 | 34.07705 | 31.76891 | 9.047679 | 28.92115 |
| p-value | 0.4201 | 0.0000** | 0.0001** | 0.3383 | 0.0003** |
| Agriculture | **D_agriaid** | **D_dpriv** | **D_dtrade** | **D_sav** | **D_gov** |
| Coefficient-β | -15572.01 | -12200.23 | -5242.691 | 1674.624 | 260.021 |
| $\chi^2$ | 7.509543 | 21.74562 | 11.96838 | 9.22967 | 45.33029 |
| p-value | 0.4828 | 0.0054** | 0.1526 | 0.3233 | 0.0000** |
| Education | **Deducaid** | **D_dpriv** | **D_dtrade** | **D_sav** | **D_gov** |
| Coefficient-β | -4705.957 | 81.97008 | 271.0293 | -378.8908 | 22.42045 |
| $\chi^2$ | 49.9869 | 17.89058 | 10.29417 | 13.88936 | 48.25542 |
| p-value | 0.0000** | 0.0221* | 0.2450 | 0.0847 | 0.0000** |
| Health Sector | **D_healaid** | **D_dpriv** | **D_dtrade** | **D_sav** | **D_gov** |
| Coefficient-β | -17.04431 | 12.70707 | 17.86084 | -5.621293 | -37.49298 |
| $\chi^2$ | 13.49253 | 14.36846 | 11.45907 | 18.48906 | 89.47895 |
| p-value | 0.0960 | 0.0727 | 0.1770 | 0.0178* | 0.0000** |

**Note: *** denotes rejection of the null hypothesis at 1% level of significance.**

The estimated long run growth equation of aggregate level is describes as follows. That is;

$$Drealgdp = 4786.74Dfaid - 21408.56Ddpriv - 4930.17Dtrade - 2370.38Dsav + 2605.55Dgov. \quad (22)$$

(8.1378) (34.0770) (31.7689) (9.0476) (28.9211)

(0.4201) (0.0000) ** (0.0001) ** (0.3383) (0.0003) **

Similarly, the equations of the agriculture, education and health GDP respectively are:

$$Dagdp = 15572.01\text{Dagriaid} + 12200.23\text{Ddpriv} + 5242.69\text{Ddtrade} - 1674.62\text{Dsav} - 206.02\text{Dgov}\ldots (23)$$

49.9869 17.89058 10.29417 13.88936 48.25542

(0.4828) (0.0054) ** (0.1526) (0.3233) (0.0000) **

$$Dedgdp = 4705.95\text{Deducaid} - 81.97\text{Ddpriv} - 271.02\text{Ddtrade} + 378.89\text{Dsav} - 22.42\text{Dgov}\ldots(24)$$

49.9869 17.89058 10.29417 13.88936 48.25542

(0.0000)** (0.0221)* (0.2450) (0.0847) (0.0000) **

$$Dhegdp = 17.04\text{Dagriaid} - 12.70\text{Ddpriv} - 17.86\text{Ddtrade} + 5.62\text{Dsav} + 37.49\text{Dgov}.\ldots\ldots\ldots.(25)$$

13.49253 14.36846 11.45907 18.48906 89.47895

(0.0960) (0.0727) (0.1770) (0.0178)* (0.0000) **

As shown in the above equations, the long run result depicts those most explanatory variables such as private capital flows, openness to trade and government expenditure are significant in affecting aggregate GDP growth at one percent level of significance and the remaining are not. At the sectoral level government expenditure for the three sectors and private capital follows for agriculture and educational sector are significant in affecting their respective GDP growth.

The result of the above equation (22 to 25) shows foreign aid is found to have a positive and but insignificant impact on aggregate real GDP, agricultural and health GDP i.e. a one percent increment of respective aid leads to a large amount increment in aggregate real GDP and sectoral GDP whereas educational sector aid is found to have a positively and statistically significant impact on educational GDP. The result showed that educational foreign aid has played an important role in promoting domestic capital formation, and has been used effectively for financing domestic investment projects among other. The result can be taken as an argument for the view that aid affects growth through its effect on human capital investment.

Moreover, the result of the study shows that private capital flow in Ethiopia has significant at 1percent of significance level but have negative impact on real GDP growth at aggregate level and positive for agricultural sector GDP. This suggests that despite resource gaps are closed through private capital flows from foreign capital, private capital flows has adverse impact on real GDP growth of the country and hence enhances the agricultural sector GDP. Also, private capital flow of has insignificant at 1percent level of significance but negative. This also suggests that even though resource gaps are closed through private capital flows, it does not has adverse effect on education and health sector GDP growth of the country. Furthermore, the capital gained through private capital flows that otherwise would be paid is used effectively to promote economic growth of the country.

The other variable that was considered in the growth equation was openness to trade. It is highly associated with the out and in flows of financial resource that includes aid flows. It was significant but negative at aggregate level for real GDP growth. This implies that despite trade can fill resources required for economic growth; it can adversely affect the aggregate economic growth of the country. The effect of openness to trade is insignificant at the sectoral level but positive for agriculture and negative for education and health sector. This further reveals that openness to trade promotes agricultural sector GDP growth and adversely affects the GDP growth of education and health sector of the country.

Domestic saving also entered in the long run growth equation. The result of the study shows that there is statistically insignificant result for aggregate and sectoral level of the economy at 1percent level of significance and has negative sign for aggregate real GDP and agricultural sector GDP growth. However, it shows positive effect educational and health sector GDP growth. The finding is not in line with the theoretical expectation and indicated that domestic capital has not served to promote investment in the country which in turn affects economic growth of the country. It is commonly believed that saving is a source of funding for investment in the economy. Any policy that is designed to stimulate saving, will also stimulate investment that leads to economic growth.

From the finding of the study, it is possible to argue that domestic capital (saving) has not been allocated for productive investment activities, and /or the poor development and policy of the financial sector has constrained saving from fostering investment that in turn enhances economic growth. This has a far reaching implication for the country in terms of dependency on foreign capital, poverty reduction and promoting economic growth of the country. On the other hand, the result may appear to indicate the fact that inflow of foreign capital retarded and created a downward pressure on domestic saving which diminishes the positive effect and leads to a negative relationship between saving and real GDP growth of Ethiopia.

Finally, the study reveals that government expenditure has significant for both aggregate and sectoral level and has positive sign for aggregate real GDP and health sector at 1percent significance level. However, it has negative for agricultural and educational GDP growth. This reveals that government expenditure is the main determinant factor for economic growth at all level and they are complimentary to each other. Furthermore, the effects of government expenditure adversely affect the growth of agricultural and educational sector than health and aggregate level GDP growth of the country. This was in line with the theory that suggests government expenditure fosters economic growth of a given country.

### 3.2.3. Short Run VECM Estimation of Economic Growth

Vector error correction model captures both the long run and the short run dynamics relationship. While the change in the output from the short run out put represents a variation in the short run, the coefficient of the error correction term captures the speed of adjustment towards the long run relationship.

Given that the variables constituting the growth equation are found to be co-integrating, the next step is estimating a vector error correction model for economic growth equations. As it is evident from the long run equilibrium growth equations, all variables except real GDP growth are endogenously determined in the system. Augmented Dickey Fuller test was used to test for stationary of the residuals (ECTs) and the result exhibit it is stationary at I(0) and I(1). Therefore there exists a relationship between the endogenous variables in the system.

**Table 17: Stationary of error correction terms in aggregate and sectors**

| Variables | ADF test | 1% CV | 5% CV | MacKinnon p-value | Stationary at |
|---|---|---|---|---|---|
| ECTgdp | -3.163* | -3.716 | -2.986 | 0.0223 | I(0) |
| ECTagri | -2.505 | -3.716 | -2.986 | 0.1143 | |
| ECTagri-1 | -4.732** | -3.723 | -2.989 | 0.0001 | I(1) |
| ECTedu | -3.234* | -3.709 | -2.983 | 0.0181 | I(0) |
| ECThel | -3.025* | -3.709 | -2.983 | 0.0326 | I(0) |

**** And * represent variables are significant at 1percent and 5percent Mackinnon critical values for rejection of haypothesis of a unit root respectively. ECTgdp, ECTagri, ECTedu, and ECThel are ECT of real GDP, agriculture, education and health GDP respectively.**

The result of the study reveals that the independent variables explain nearly 82.3 percent of the change in dynamic model of real GDP growth equation. The tests confirmed that the model is well specified and the regression analysis is adequate. The diagnostic tests show that the null of tests are not rejected except for the joint insignificance of the explanatory variables i.e. the coefficients of the explanatory variables are jointly significant. The optimal lag length is determined at lag length of two using Akakie Information Criteria (AIC). Table 18 to 19 summarizes the results of dynamic growth equation for real GDP, agricultural GDP, education GDP and health GDP respectively.

**Table 18: Result for dynamic growth equation for real GDP**

| Dynamic growth equation of real GDP | | | Growth equation of Agricultural GDP | | |
|---|---|---|---|---|---|
| Variable | Coef. | P-Value | Variable | Coef. | P-Value |
| drealgdp | 2.255596 | 0.332 | dagriaid | 18180.61 | 0.306 |
| dfaid | 1396.834 | 0.515 | dpriv | -16964.41** | 0.027 |
| dpriv | -3822.32 | 0.252 | dtrade | -740.4071 | 0.788 |
| dtrade | -569.9935 | 0.670 | dsav | -868.2708 | 0.746 |
| dsav | -704.0366 | 0.549 | dgov | 24031.92*** | 0.000 |
| dgov | 8957.272 | 0.126 | ECTagri-1 | 3.377107* | 0.067 |
| ECTgdp-1 | 1.525357 | 0.423 | t_dummy | 25367.87 | 0.205 |
| t_dummy | 16831.27* | 0.069 | _cons | 2905.942 | 0.844 |
| _cons | 37646.09*** | 0.000 | | | |
| R-squared= 0.8231, Adj R-squared= 0.7558, F( 8, 21)= 12.22 (0.0000)**** | | | R-squared = 0.7479, Adj R-squared =0.6676, F( 7, 22)= 9.32 (0.0000)*** | | |

**Note: ***, ** and * denotes significance at 1percent 5percent and 10percent respectively**

The sectoral dynamic growth equation test result reveals that the independent variables explain nearly74.9 percent, 94.3 percent and, 93.0 percent of the change in dynamic model of agriculture, education, and health GDP growth equations respectively. The test results confirmed that the model is well specified and the regression analysis is adequate. The diagnostic tests show that the null of tests are not rejected except for the joint insignificance of the explanatory variables i.e. the coefficients of the explanatory variables are jointly significant. The optimal lag length is determined at lag length of two using AIC.

**Table 19: Result for dynamic growth equation for educational and health GDP**

| Growth equation for educational GDP | | | Growth equation for Health GDP | | |
|---|---|---|---|---|---|
| Variable | Coef. | P-Value | Variable | Coef. | P-Value |
| deducaid | 544.0046** | 0.025 | dhealaid | 106.0769 | 0.172 |
| dpriv | -689.5291*** | 0.000 | dpriv | -147.8256*** | 0.003 |
| dtrade | -113.6063** | 0.045 | dtrade | -34.35791* | 0.088 |
| dsav | -483.4148*** | 0.000 | dsav | -31.28777 | 0.117 |
| dgov | 1590.149*** | 0.000 | dgov | 346.1991*** | 0.000 |
| ECTedu-1 | 4.970953*** | 0.000 | ECThel-1 | 3.098025*** | 0.000 |
| t_dummy | 92.87297 | 0.822 | t_dummy | 280.1963* | 0.058 |
| _cons | 228.3693 | 0.423 | _cons | 60.76483 | 0.557 |
| R-squared = 0.9438<br>Adj R-squared =0.9267<br>F( 7, 23)= 55.22 (0.0000)*** | | | R-squared=0.9301,<br>Adj R-squared=0.9088, and<br>F( 7, 23)= 43.70(0.0000)*** | | |

**Note: ***and ** denotes significance at 1percent and 5percent respectively**

The estimated dynamic equation for real GDP growth result indicates that official development assistance has insignificant effect on growth at an aggregate level, agriculture, and health but significant for education sector GDP growth. The finding point that foreign aid is used to finance investment activity (particularly in human capital) which has a longer gestation period and its impact may not be reflected in the short run.

Major political change from the Derg to EPRDF (D91) has an immediate positive impact on real GDP and sectoral GDP growth. However, the long run effects of such change are not analyzed since the objective was to identify the immediate short run effect of political unrest. The coefficient of major shifts in government from the Derg regime to EPRDF (D91) is not statistically significant except for health sector even though it has a positive sign. The error correcting term is statistically significant for real GDP, education and health at 1percent level of significance and at 10 percent level of significance for agricultural sector GDP growth.

### 3.2.4. Causality Analysis of Aggregate and Sectoral Economic Growth

The relationship between economic output (GDP) and foreign aid remains one of the controversial areas in macroeconomics. At the heart of the debate lies the question of "causation", and whether it is "GDP growth that causes foreign aid" or "foreign aid that causes

GDP growth", or whether there exist bidirectional causality between the two variables. The presence and direction of causality between real GDP and official development assistance as well as sectoral GDP and sector specific aid is tested in this sub-section.

However, the approach used is different from the standard Granger-causality test which is based on VAR analysis. According to Granger (1998) cited in Tasew (2011), if cointegration is detected between the variables, then Granger causality must be conducted in VECM to avoid the problem of misspecification (Tasew, 2011). Following this VECM, causality test is performed to identify the presence and direction of causality.

If real GDP (or sectoral GDP) and foreign aid (sectoral aid) are co-integrated, the finding of no causality in either direction is unacceptable. Since cointegration says nothing about the direction of causality, it is mandatory to estimate a VECM from the long run co-integrating vectors to detect the direction of causation. In addition, using VEC model to detect causality enables to distinguish between short-run and long-run causality. According to Boon (2000) short run causality is reflected through the coefficients of differences of the lagged explanatory variables, whereas the long run causality is implied through the coefficient (adjustment parameter) of the lagged error correction terms which contains the long-run information (Boon, 2000).

The unit root test performed in this study indicated that both variables are stationary and it is possible to proceed to test for long run relationship using the Johansen's co-integration test approach. The test result revealed that there is one cointegrating vector, and points to estimate a VECM to test for causality. The result is obtained at lag length of one by the information criteria and hence only one lag is used to test for cointegration and in the estimation of VECM. The result of the test shows that there is a single unique co-integrating vector constituting the long run relationship between real GDP (sectoral GDP) and aid (sectoral aid).

The Johansen co-integration tests for the causality test detection result of aggregate real GDP and sectoral GDP growth with total aid and sectoral aid analysis of variables reveals that the null of no co-integration is rejected at 1percent level of significance whereas the alternative hypothesis that at least one cointegrating vector is not rejected by both λmax and λtrace statistics. This suggests that there is a precisely cointegrating vector in the estimated model.

The VECM enables to capture the short run dynamics of the model and formulated based on the identified long run relationships. The cointegrating term is known as the ECT since the deviation from long run equilibrium is corrected gradually through a series of partial short run adjustments. Thus cointegration implies the presence of error correcting representation and any deviation from equilibrium will revert back to its long run path. VECM is estimated to discriminate the short run and long run causality between the variables. The result of the cointegration is computed based on equation 20A and 20B for aggregate real GDP and total foreign aid.

**Table 20: Johansen cointegration tests for the causality test detection**

| Ho: (null hypothesis) | Cointegration test between real GDP and foreign aid | | | | | | |
|---|---|---|---|---|---|---|---|
| | Eigen value ($\lambda_i$) | λmax Statistic | critical value 5% | critical value 1% | λtrace Statistic | critical value 5% | critical value 1% |
| r= 0 | | 20.5860 | 14.07 | 18.63 | 23.6503 | 15.41 | 20.04 |
| r=1 | 0.49651 | 3.0643* | 3.76 | 6.65 | 3.0643* | 3.76 | 6.65 |
| r=2 | 0.09710 | | | | | | |
| **Cointegration test between agricultural GDP and agricultural sector aid** | | | | | | | |
| r= 0 | | 37.7912 | 14.07 | 18.63 | 39.5522 | 15.41 | 20.04 |
| r=1 | 0.71626 | 1.7610* | 3.76 | 6.65 | 1.7610* | 3.76 | 6.65 |
| r=2 | 0.05701 | | | | | | |
| **Cointegration test between education GDP and educational sector foreign aid** | | | | | | | |
| r= 0 | | 47.4822 | 14.07 | 18.63 | 48.6010 | 15.41 | 20.04 |
| r=1 | 0.79459 | 1.1189* | 3.76 | 6.65 | 1.1189* | 3.76 | 6.65 |
| r=2 | 0.03661 | | | | | | |
| **Cointegration test between health GDP and health sector foreign aid** | | | | | | | |
| r= 0 | | 44.5718 | 14.07 | 18.63 | 63.2232 | 15.41 | 20.04 |
| r=1 | 0.77366 | 18.65138 | 3.76 | 6.65 | 18.6513 | 3.76 | 6.65 |
| r=2 | 0.46298 | | | | | | |

**** denotes significance at 1percent significance level**

Similarly, for the sectoral level, equation 21A and 21B is used in the estimation. An F-test is conducted on the coefficients of the lagged difference terms of both equations at aggregate and sectoral level to identify the presence of short run causality. On the other hand, absence of long run causality necessitates the coefficients of the error correcting term to be zero for the respective equations. A zero restriction is made on the adjustment parameters to test the null of no long run causality. The test result shows real GDP does not Granger cause foreign aid and the converse does not hold. Therefore, aid does not granger cause real GDP at aggregate level of Ethiopian economic growth.

The test result also reveals that health and agricultural GDP of Ethiopia does not granger cause health aid and agricultural sector aid. The result further points not only the absence of short run causality from agricultural GDP to aid but also the adjustment parameter is not significant even at 10 percent significance level and the result is inconclusive. It is only the educational aid that granger causes educational GDP in the short run as well as in the long run of Ethiopian economic growth.

**Table 21: Causality test between GDP and aid at aggregate and sectoral level**

| Hypothesis | Dependent Variable | | Adjustment parameter | |
|---|---|---|---|---|
| | Value | F-test | Value | F-test |
| Real GDP does not granger cause foreign aid | .022591 | 0.606 | -.1597665 | 0.248 |
| Foreign aid does not granger cause real GDP | .0142104 | 0.826 | .0000378 | 0.714 |
| Agricultural GDP does not granger cause agricultural foreign aid | .4410527 | 0.000** | -.3104556 | 0.301 |
| Agricultural aid does not granger cause agricultural GDP | .0143196 | 0.773 | -9.75e-06 | 0.615 |
| Educational GDP does not granger cause educational foreign aid | .0136216 | 0.192 | -.0295338 | 0.644 |
| Educational aid does not granger cause educational GDP | -1.081689 | 0.000** | -.0003668 | 0.022* |
| Health GDP does not granger cause health sector foreign aid | .0155432 | 0.463 | -.0767071 | 0.456 |
| Health sector aid does not granger cause health GDP | .0215541 | 0.746 | .0003388 | 0.664 |

**** And * denote F-statistics significance at 1 percent and 5 percent. A lag length of two is used for the estimation of VECM.**

Educational aid causes educational sector GDP growth in the short run at 1percent significance level. Also the significance of the adjustment parameter indicates the presence of long run causality from aid to educational GDP. Thus there exists bidirectional causality from aid to educational GDP and vice-versa.

# CHAPTER FOUR: SUMMARY AND CONCLUSION

## 4.1. Summary

Foreign aid remained an important source of finance for capital scarce (poor) countries and continued to play a multifaceted role in financing their development needs. Despite the massive literature on the subject, a consensus has not been reached by researchers regarding the growth impact of aid, rather the results are inconclusive. Thus one can find both success and failure stories.

The study has examined the macroeconomic of Ethiopia with special emphasis given to the impact of foreign aid on domestic capital formation, economic growth, and external trade, as well as its nature and composition of country's expenditure and type and trends of foreign aid at aggregate and sectoral level to the country. The study makes an effort to establish whether there exists long run and short run relationship between foreign aid & growth with an annual data covering the period 1981 to 2012. For these purpose growth equations of vector auto regression method is estimated. Multivariate co-integration technique is used for the analysis of the long run relation whereas VECM analysis is used in the assessment of the short run relationships and its linkage with the long run equilibrium path.

Since cointegration necessitates the variables to be stationery, the series is tested for unit root and the result found indicated that certain variables are stationary at level and others become stationary after first difference i.e. I(0) and I(1). As a result, we run a test for co-integration on the equations and the result suffice the presence of long run relationship among the variables in the model. The result from the growth equation revealed that aid contributed positively to economic growth both at aggregate and sectoral level in the long run and particularly significant in education. However, its short run effect appeared insignificant for aggregate real GDP, agriculture, and health sectors.

Causality tests among pairs of variables of interest are addressed in growth equation. The presence and direction of causality between variables in the growth equation is conducted based on VECM. A VECM is used to facilitate the discrimination of the short run and long run causality among the variables. The causality test result between educational GDP and educational foreign aid indicates the existence of bi-directional causality between educational GDP and educational foreign aid. There is also a unidirectional causality between agricultural aid and agricultural GDP growth. The result of the study is in line dominant theoretical views point that aid modality which is aimed to facilitate micro-aspect of foreign aid than macro aspect of aid donation.

## 4.2. Conclusion

Foreign aid remained an important source of finance for capital scarce countries & continued in financing their development needs. Also, the result from the growth equation revealed that aid contributed positively to economic growth both at aggregate and sectoral level in the long run and particularly significant in education, but its short run effect appeared insignificant for aggregate real GDP, agriculture and health sectors. The causality test result between educational GDP and educational sector foreign aid indicates the existence of bi-directional causality between the two variables. This implies that the result of the study an evident that it is in line dominant theoretical views point that aid modality which is aimed to facilitate micro-aspect of foreign aid than macro aspect of aid donation.

## 4.3. Policy Implication

The empirical results found in this study have some important policy implications for policy makers and researchers in the areas of foreign aid. Even though aid appeared to have a significant role in financing economic growth of developing countries like Ethiopia in the long run, sectoral analysis of the impact of foreign aid on economic growth of the country is indispensible. Some mechanisms have to be designed to motivate researchers and policy makers of the country to have a deep insight about the importance of its impact at sectoral level for efficient and effective utilization of foreign aid the way to minimize reliance on foreign aid through;

- Enhancing the domestic revenue raising capacity of the country which is at the heart of the mechanism to meet the capital required for the economy in times of short falls of external resources.
- Ethiopian government has to set a sound macroeconomic policy environment which stimulates economic growth that is adequate enough to finance the economy of the country.
- The country has to reduce the long run dependency on foreign aid to cater the increasing demand of development and also to mitigate the exposition of the country to external shocks,
- Ethiopia has to expand its domestic tax base of the economy along with good institutions that can combat fraud and corruption in the process of tax collection. The revenue from an extensive tax base enables the country to finance its expenditure on domestic capital and hence less dependence on foreign aid to meet the development needs

## Reference

Abuzeid, F. (2009). Foreign Aid and the "Big Push" Theory: Lessons from Sub-Saharan Africa. *Stanford Journal of International Relations , 11* (1), 16-23.

Arellano, C., Bulíř, A., Lane, T., & Lipschitz, L. (2009). The dynamic implications of foreign aid and its variability. *Journal of Development Economics , 88*, 87–102.

Bakare, A. (2011). The Macroeconomic Impact of Foreign Aid in Sub-Sahara Africa: The Case of Nigeria. *Business and Management Review , 1* (5), 24 – 32.

Benedek, D., Crivelli, E., Gupta, S., & Muthoora, P. (2012, July). Foreign Aid and Revenue: Still a Crowding Out Effect? *International Monetary Fund Working Paper WP/12/186 .*

Bhattarai, B. P. (2007). Foreign Aid and Government's Fiscal Behaviour in Nepal: An Empirical Analysis. *Economic Analysis & Policy , 37* (1), 41-60.

Boon, T. (2000). Saving, investment and capital flows: an empirical study of the Asian economies. *working paper 3.2000 .*

Burnside, C., & Dollar, D. (2000). Aid, Policies and Growth. *American Economic Review , 90* (4), 847-868.

Bwire, T., Morrissey, O., & Lloyda, T. (2013, March ). The Fiscal Impact of Aid in Uganda: An Application of a Cointegrated Vector Autoregressive model. *Bank of Uganda Working Paper No. 07/2013 .*

Chenery, H. B., & Strout, A. M. (1966). Foreign assistance and economic development. *American Economic Review* ( 56), 680–733.

Durbarry, R., Gemmell, N., & Greenaway, D. (1998). New Evidence on the Impact of Foreign Aid on Economic Growth. *Centre for Research in Economic Development and International Trade Research Paper No. 98/8 .*

Enders, W. (1995). *Applied Econometric Time Series* . New York: John Wiley and Sons Inc .

Eroglu, O., & Yavaz, A. (2005). The Role of Foreign Aid in Economic Development of Developing Countries. *Suleyman Demirel University, Turkey* , 144-158.

Gebhard, N., Kitterman, K., Mitchell, A. A., Nielson, D., & Wilson, S. ( 2008). Healthy Aid: Preliminary Results on Health Aid Effectiveness August 28-31. *The annual meeting of the American Political Science Association* (pp. 1-27). Boston, Massachusetts: Brigham Young University.

Granger, C. (1969). Investigating causal relations by econometric models and crossspectral methods. *Econometrica , 37* (3), 424–438.

Gujarati, D. (1995). *Basic Econometrics* (3 ed.). Mc Graw-Hill, Inc.

Gujarati, D. (2004). *Basic Econometrics* (4 ed.). New York: McGraw-Hill Companies.

Harris, R. ( 1995). *Using Cointegration Analysis in Econometric Modeling.* England: Simon and Schuster International Group.

Hayakawa, K. (2011). *An Improved GMM Estimation of Panel VAR Models with Applications to Granger Causality Test and Impulse Response Analysis.* Department of Economics, Hiroshima University.

Kumler'07, T. J. (2007, April 27). The Impact of Foreign Aid on Development and Aggregate Welfare in Developing Countries. *Economics Department Honors Projects Paper 19 .*

Leeson, P. T. (2008). Escaping Poverty: Foreign Aid, Private Property, and Economic Development. *The Journal of Private Enterprise , 23* (2), 39-64.

Lohani'04, S. (2004, April 22). Effect of Foreign Aid on Development: Does More Money Bring More Development? *Research Honors Paper Projects Paper 18. Department ofEconomics Illinois Wesleyan University .*

M'Amanja, D., Lloyd, T., & Morrissey, O. (2005). Fiscal Aggregates, Aid and Growth in Kenya: A Vector Autoregressive (VAR) Analysis. *Centre for Research in Economic Development and International Trade Research Paper No. 05/07 .*

Marc., L. (2014, January 18). The Causal Links between Aid and Government Expenditures. *Tinbergen Institute Discussion Paper TI 2014-012/V .*

Martins, P. M. (2010). *Essays on the Macroeconomic Management of Foreign Aid Flows in Africa: Research submitted for the degree of Doctor of Philosophy in Economics.* Brighton, United Kingdom: Institute of Development Studies University of Sussex.

McGillivray, M., Feeny, S., Hermes, N., & Lensink, R. (2005, August). It Works; It Doesn't;It Can, But That Depends…50 Years of Controversy over the Macroeconomic Impact of Development Aid . *United Nations University -WIDER Research Paper 2005/54 .*

MoFED. (2011). *Annual Report on Macroeconomic Development EFY 2002 (2009/10).* Addis Ababa, Ethiopia: Macro Economy Policy and Manegement Directrote.

Moreira, S. B. (2005). Evaluating the Impact of Foreign Aid on Economic Growth: A Cross-Country Study. *Journal of Economic Development , 30* (2), 24-49.

Nganwa, P. (2013, February). Resources for poverty eradication: A background paper. *Development Initiatives: Africa hub Ethiopia* .

Odusanya, I., Abidemi, L., & Akanni, L. (2011). Foreign aid, public expenditure and economic growth: The Nigerian case. *The Journal of Applied Business Research , 27* (3), 33-42.

OECD. (2009). *Manaing Aid, Better Aid: Practices of DAC Member Countries.* France: OECD Publishing.

Pattillo, C., Polak, J., & Roy, J. (2007, June ). Measuring the Effect of Foreign Aid on Growth and Poverty Reduction or The Pitfalls of Interaction Variables. *International Monetary Fund Working Paper WP/ 07/145* .

Paul, J., & Pistor, M. (2009, May 13). Official Development Spending. *Parliamentary Information and Research Service PRP 07-10E* , 1-5.

Pettersson, J. (2007). Foreign Sectoral Aid Fungibility: Growth and Poverty Reduction. *Journal of International Development , 19* (8), 1074–1098.

Prizzon, A., & Rogerson, A. (2013). *The age of choice:Ethiopia in the new aid landscape.* London: Overseas Development Institute.

Radelet, S. (2006, July). A Primer on Foreign Aid: Working Paper Number 92. *Center for Global Development* , 1-24.

Ram, R. (1986). Government size and economic growth: a new framework and some evidence from cross-section and time-series data. *American Economic Review , 76* (1).

Randhawa, G. K. (2012). Foreign Aid in Economic Development. *International Journal of Computing & Business Research* , 1-10.

Shah, S. A., Ahmad, I., & Zahid, M. S. (2005). Is Foreign Aid Necessary for the Economic Development of Less Developed Countries with Special Reference to Pakistan? *IPRI Journal , v* (2), 1-27.

Tasew, T. (2011). Foreign Aid and Economic Growth in Ethiopia:A Cointegration Analysis. *The Economiic Researrch Guarrdiian ) , 1* (2), 88-108.

Todaro, M. P., & Smith, S. C. (2012). *Economic Development* (11th ed.). New York: Pearson Education, Inc. .

Tofik, S. (2012). Official development assistance (ODA), public spending and economic growth in Ethiopia. *Journal of Economics and International Finance , 4* (8), 173-191.

UNCTAD. (2006). Doubling Aid: Making the "Big Push" work. *Economic Development in Africa* (pp. 1-107). New York and Geneva: United Nations publication.

USAID. (2003). *Ethiopia fact sheet, No. 10.* Washington, DC.: United States Agency for International Development .

WB. (1998). *Assessing aid: what works, what doesn't and why A World Bank Policy Research Report.* USA: Oxford University Press.

World Bank. (2013). *Africa Development Indicators 2012/13.* Washington, DC: World Bank.

Zhou, Z., Bonham, C., & Gangnes. (2007). Modeling the supply and demand for Tourism: a fully identified VECM approach, working paper No.07-17.

# Appendixes

### Appendex-1 Sample sectoral ODA flow to Ethiopia from DAC donor

**Dataset: GeoBook: ODA by sector – bilateral commitments by donor and recipient**

| **Donor** | DAC Countries, Total | | | | | | |
|---|---|---|---|---|---|---|---|
| **Recipient** | Ethiopia | | | | | | |
| **Year** | 2006 | 2007 | 2008 | 2009 | 2010 | 2011 | 2012 |
| **Sector** | | | | | | | |
| Bilateral ODA Commitments by Purpose (CRS) | 999.46 | 1061.44 | 2059.27 | 2192.13 | 1839.77 | 1739.33 | 1896.24 |
| Social Infrastructure & Services | 593.63 | 584.45 | 830.8 | 1135.41 | 659.06 | 660.93 | 893.62 |
| Education | 269.49 | 74.24 | 126.59 | 394.88 | 125.76 | 185.67 | 266.04 |
| Water Supply And Sanitation | 24.31 | 61.91 | 161.5 | 119.41 | 47.68 | 67.94 | 39.83 |
| Economic Infrastructure and Services | 32.17 | 23.25 | 31.88 | 112.16 | 48.83 | 156.73 | 49.05 |
| Transport and Communications | 5.19 | 11.06 | 2.65 | 4.57 | 14.25 | 71.57 | 4.03 |
| Energy | 0.36 | 0.57 | 1.34 | 86.36 | 5.11 | 79.26 | 17.48 |
| Production Sectors | 24.26 | 69.73 | 80.98 | 77.17 | 187.44 | 122.28 | 281.21 |
| Agriculture, Forestry & Fishing | 21.54 | 66.57 | 43.08 | 70.54 | 177.59 | 108.97 | 274.47 |
| Industry, Mining & Construction | 2.31 | 2.07 | 36.86 | 3.22 | 6.88 | 12.04 | 4.81 |
| Trade and Tourism | 0.41 | 1.1 | 1.04 | 3.42 | 2.98 | 1.27 | 1.93 |
| Multisector | 35.56 | 53.57 | 59.98 | 70.77 | 116.29 | 48.51 | 121.17 |
| Programme Assistance | 58.7 | 60.43 | 291.6 | 176.38 | 292.01 | 179.45 | 177.77 |
| Food Aid | 49.48 | 60.43 | 291.58 | 159.25 | 285.29 | 179.45 | 177.77 |
| Action Relating to Debt | 28.35 | 2.51 | 0.54 | 0.06 | 0.05 | 0.04 | 0.03 |
| Humanitarian Aid | 215.07 | 260.54 | 751.96 | 608.03 | 518.58 | 564.6 | 359.54 |
| Unallocated/Unspecified | 11.71 | 6.94 | 11.54 | 12.13 | 17.5 | 6.78 | 13.85 |

data extracted on 29 Apr 2014 15:11 UTC (GMT) from OECD.Stat

**Annex 2: Results of sample time serious data**

**I, Regression result of aggregate Real GDP for testing model adequacy by R-squared**

```
. regress realgdp faid dpriv dtrade sav gov

      Source |       SS       df       MS              Number of obs =      31
-------------+------------------------------           F(  5,    25) =  185.22
       Model |  3.9199e+10     5  7.8399e+09           Prob > F      =  0.0000
    Residual |  1.0582e+09    25  42328408.7           R-squared     =  0.9737
-------------+------------------------------           Adj R-squared =  0.9685
       Total |  4.0258e+10    30  1.3419e+09           Root MSE      =    6506

------------------------------------------------------------------------------
     realgdp |      Coef.   Std. Err.      t    P>|t|     [95% Conf. Interval]
-------------+----------------------------------------------------------------
        faid |  -671.9655   354.3998    -1.90   0.070    -1401.866    57.93464
       dpriv |  -1029.447   1001.558    -1.03   0.314    -3092.193      1033.3
      dtrade |   189.1482    394.372     0.48   0.636    -623.0761    1001.372
         sav |  -1106.754   396.6634    -2.79   0.010    -1923.698   -289.8103
         gov |   2709.163   107.2899    25.25   0.000     2488.195    2930.131
       _cons |   35329.82   5353.155     6.60   0.000     24304.79    46354.85

. vif

    Variable |       VIF       1/VIF
-------------+----------------------
        faid |      1.62    0.615675
         gov |      1.53    0.655619
       dpriv |      1.50    0.667980
      dtrade |      1.31    0.763653
         sav |      1.23    0.810134
-------------+----------------------
    Mean VIF |      1.44
```

**II, Sample of variable that is stationarity with drift and trend included in ADF at level**

```
. dfuller realgdp

Dickey-Fuller test for unit root                   Number of obs   =        31

                               ---------- Interpolated Dickey-Fuller ---------
                  Test         1% Critical       5% Critical      10% Critical
               Statistic           Value             Value             Value
------------------------------------------------------------------------------
 Z(t)              7.363            -3.709            -2.983            -2.623
------------------------------------------------------------------------------
MacKinnon approximate p-value for Z(t) = 1.0000
```

**III, Sample of variable that is non stationarity at level but stationary after first differencing (the cause of openness to trade)**

```
. dfuller trade

Dickey-Fuller test for unit root                   Number of obs   =        31

                               ---------- Interpolated Dickey-Fuller ---------
                  Test         1% Critical       5% Critical      10% Critical
               Statistic           Value             Value             Value
------------------------------------------------------------------------------
 Z(t)             -0.434            -3.709            -2.983            -2.623
------------------------------------------------------------------------------
MacKinnon approximate p-value for Z(t) = 0.9042

. dfuller dtrade

Dickey-Fuller test for unit root                   Number of obs   =        30

                               ---------- Interpolated Dickey-Fuller ---------
                  Test         1% Critical       5% Critical      10% Critical
               Statistic           Value             Value             Value
------------------------------------------------------------------------------
 Z(t)             -5.033            -3.716            -2.986            -2.624
------------------------------------------------------------------------------
MacKinnon approximate p-value for Z(t) = 0.0000
```

**IV, Sample example for Johansen test for co-integration in real GDP growth equation**

```
. vecrank realgdp faid  dpriv dtrade sav gov, trend(constant) max levela

                      Johansen tests for cointegration
Trend: constant                                         Number of obs =      29
Sample:  1984 - 2012                                             Lags =       2
-------------------------------------------------------------------------------
maximum                                      trace    5% critical  1% critical
  rank    parms       LL       eigenvalue  statistic     value        value
    0      42    -585.11429                122.4099      94.15       103.18
    1      53    -563.72697     0.77122     79.6352      68.52        76.07
    2      62    -547.09203     0.68249     46.3653*1*5  47.21        54.46
    3      69    -536.05935     0.53274     24.3000      29.68        35.65
    4      74    -528.94219     0.38789     10.0657      15.41        20.04
    5      77    -524.87975     0.24434      1.9408       3.76         6.65
    6      78    -523.90935     0.06473
-------------------------------------------------------------------------------
maximum                                        max    5% critical  1% critical
  rank    parms       LL       eigenvalue  statistic     value        value
    0      42    -585.11429                 42.7746      39.37        45.10
    1      53    -563.72697     0.77122     33.2699      33.46        38.77
    2      62    -547.09203     0.68249     22.0653      27.07        32.24
    3      69    -536.05935     0.53274     14.2343      20.97        25.52
    4      74    -528.94219     0.38789      8.1249      14.07        18.63
    5      77    -524.87975     0.24434      1.9408       3.76         6.65
    6      78    -523.90935     0.06473
-------------------------------------------------------------------------------
```

## V. Sample result of VECM for real GDP with its run alpha and beta coefficients

```
. vec realgdp faid dpriv dtrade sav gov, trend(constant) alpha dforce
```

Vector error-correction model

| Sample: 1984 - 2012 | | No. of obs | = 29 |
|---|---|---|---|
| | | AIC | = 42.53289 |
| Log likelihood = | -563.727 | HQIC | = 43.3155 |
| Det(Sigma_ml) = | 3.09e+09 | SBIC | = 45.03175 |

| Equation | Parms | RMSE | R-sq | chi2 | P>chi2 |
|---|---|---|---|---|---|
| D_realgdp | 8 | 3504.6 | 0.8197 | 95.45467 | 0.0000 |
| D_faid | 8 | 2.32222 | 0.2789 | 8.121136 | 0.4217 |
| D_dpriv | 8 | 1.5036 | 0.6196 | 34.198 | 0.0000 |
| D_dtrade | 8 | 3.57501 | 0.6020 | 31.76664 | 0.0001 |
| D_sav | 8 | 3.49294 | 0.3014 | 9.058087 | 0.3374 |
| D_gov | 8 | 2.35581 | 0.5794 | 28.93399 | 0.0003 |

| | Coef. | Std. Err. | z | P>\|z\| | [95% Conf. | Interval] |
|---|---|---|---|---|---|---|
| **D_realgdp** | | | | | | |
| _ce1 L1. | -.071375 | .0336007 | -2.12 | 0.034 | -.1372313 | -.0055188 |
| realgdp LD. | .4291794 | .1944394 | 2.21 | 0.027 | .0480852 | .8102735 |
| faid LD. | -27.5806 | 357.0693 | -0.08 | 0.938 | -727.4236 | 672.2624 |
| dpriv LD. | 758.9282 | 467.0421 | 1.62 | 0.104 | -156.4575 | 1674.314 |
| dtrade LD. | 310.0795 | 196.3837 | 1.58 | 0.114 | -74.82549 | 694.9844 |
| sav LD. | -218.2003 | 224.4719 | -0.97 | 0.331 | -658.1572 | 221.7567 |
| gov LD. | 1011.443 | 443.0348 | 2.28 | 0.022 | 143.1105 | 1879.775 |
| _cons | .0015409 | 988.5087 | 0.00 | 1.000 | -1937.44 | 1937.443 |

Cointegrating equations

| Equation | Parms | chi2 | P>chi2 |
|---|---|---|---|
| _ce1 | 5 | 135.26 | 0.0000 |

Identification: beta is exactly identified
Johansen normalization restriction imposed

| beta | Coef. | Std. Err. | z | P>\|z\| | [95% Conf. | Interval] |
|---|---|---|---|---|---|---|
| **_ce1** | | | | | | |
| realgdp | 1 | . | . | . | . | . |
| faid | -4809.798 | 1012.468 | -4.75 | 0.000 | -6794.199 | -2825.397 |
| dpriv | 21489.63 | 4319.312 | 4.98 | 0.000 | 13023.93 | 29955.32 |
| dtrade | 4943.351 | 1233.335 | 4.01 | 0.000 | 2526.058 | 7360.644 |
| sav | 2390.033 | 1143.308 | 2.09 | 0.037 | 149.1899 | 4630.876 |
| gov | -2609.68 | 503.0852 | -5.19 | 0.000 | -3595.708 | -1623.651 |
| _cons | -20265.57 | . | . | . | . | . |

Adjustment parameters

| Equation | Parms | chi2 | P>chi2 |
|---|---|---|---|
| D_realgdp | 1 | 4.512267 | 0.0337 |
| D_faid | 1 | .6575591 | 0.4174 |
| D_dpriv | 1 | 11.30047 | 0.0008 |
| D_dtrade | 1 | 9.948582 | 0.0016 |
| D_sav | 1 | .6168383 | 0.4322 |
| D_gov | 1 | .1384403 | 0.7098 |

| alpha | Coef. | Std. Err. | z | P>\|z\| | [95% Conf. | Interval] |
|---|---|---|---|---|---|---|
| **D_realgdp** | | | | | | |
| _ce1 L1. | -.071375 | .0336007 | -2.12 | 0.034 | -.1372313 | -.0055188 |
| **D_faid** | | | | | | |
| _ce1 L1. | -.0000181 | .0000223 | -0.81 | 0.417 | -.0000617 | .0000256 |
| **D_dpriv** | | | | | | |
| _ce1 L1. | -.0000485 | .0000144 | -3.36 | 0.001 | -.0000767 | -.0000202 |
| **D_dtrade** | | | | | | |
| _ce1 L1. | -.0001081 | .0000343 | -3.15 | 0.002 | -.0001753 | -.0000409 |
| **D_sav** | | | | | | |
| _ce1 L1. | .0000263 | .0000335 | 0.79 | 0.432 | -.0000393 | .0000919 |
| **D_gov** | | | | | | |
| _ce1 L1. | 8.40e-06 | .0000226 | 0.37 | 0.710 | -.0000359 | .0000527 |

## VI. Sample normality test for aggregate real GDP growth equation

```
. vecnorm, jbera skewness kurtosis
```

Jarque-Bera test

| Equation | chi2 | df | Prob > chi2 |
|---|---|---|---|
| D_realgdp | 0.950 | 2 | 0.62176 |
| D_faid | 2.521 | 2 | 0.28350 |
| D_dpriv | 1.920 | 2 | 0.38297 |
| D_dtrade | 4.894 | 2 | 0.08653 |
| D_sav | 3.006 | 2 | 0.22245 |
| D_gov | 0.319 | 2 | 0.85271 |
| ALL | 13.610 | 12 | 0.32628 |

Skewness test

| Equation | Skewness | chi2 | df | Prob > chi2 |
|---|---|---|---|---|
| D_realgdp | -.40221 | 0.782 | 1 | 0.37655 |
| D_faid | .70242 | 2.385 | 1 | 0.12253 |
| D_dpriv | -.61534 | 1.830 | 1 | 0.17612 |
| D_dtrade | .90691 | 3.975 | 1 | 0.04617 |
| D_sav | -.60771 | 1.785 | 1 | 0.18154 |
| D_gov | .21545 | 0.224 | 1 | 0.63574 |
| ALL | | 10.981 | 6 | 0.08895 |

Kurtosis test

| Equation | Kurtosis | chi2 | df | Prob > chi2 |
|---|---|---|---|---|
| D_realgdp | 2.6266 | 0.168 | 1 | 0.68146 |
| D_faid | 3.3359 | 0.136 | 1 | 0.71194 |
| D_dpriv | 2.7278 | 0.090 | 1 | 0.76479 |
| D_dtrade | 3.8722 | 0.919 | 1 | 0.33771 |
| D_sav | 4.0053 | 1.221 | 1 | 0.26915 |
| D_gov | 2.7206 | 0.094 | 1 | 0.75876 |
| ALL | | 2.629 | 6 | 0.85377 |

## VII. Sample test for residual autocorrelation in aggregate real GDP growth equation

```
. veclmar
```

Lagrange-multiplier test

| lag | chi2 | df | Prob > chi2 |
|---|---|---|---|
| 1 | 30.9913 | 36 | 0.70558 |
| 2 | 32.9333 | 36 | 0.61523 |

H0: no autocorrelation at lag order

## VIII. Sample of Growth equation stability test

```
. vecstable

   Eigenvalue stability condition
```

| Eigenvalue | Modulus |
|---|---|
| 1 | 1 |
| 1 | 1 |
| 1 | 1 |
| 1 | 1 |
| 1 | 1 |
| .8967183 | .896718 |
| -.6226433 | .622643 |
| -.4613487 + .3355836*i* | .57049 |
| -.4613487 - .3355836*i* | .57049 |
| .2014753 + .2096578*i* | .290773 |
| .2014753 - .2096578*i* | .290773 |
| -.1602163 | .160216 |

```
   The VECM specification imposes 5 unit moduli.
```

## IX. Sample of lags length selection for real GDP growth equation

```
. varsoc realgdp, exog(faid dpriv dtrade sav gov) lutstats

   Selection-order criteria (lutstats)
   Sample:  1985 - 2012                          Number of obs      =        28
```

| lag | LL | LR | df | p | FPE | AIC | HQIC | SBIC |
|---|---|---|---|---|---|---|---|---|
| 0 | -283.41 | | | | 5.6e+07 | 17.4057 | 17.4057 | 17.4057 |
| 1 | -262.136 | 42.548* | 1 | 0.000 | 1.3e+07 | 15.9576 | 15.9721 | 16.0052 |
| 2 | -260.438 | 3.3956 | 1 | 0.065 | 1.3e+07* | 15.9077* | 15.9368* | 16.0029* |
| 3 | -260.246 | .38473 | 1 | 0.535 | 1.3e+07 | 15.9654 | 16.0091 | 16.1082 |
| 4 | -259.964 | .56345 | 1 | 0.453 | 1.4e+07 | 16.0167 | 16.0749 | 16.207 |

```
   Endogenous:  realgdp
    Exogenous:  faid dpriv dtrade sav gov  _cons
```

## X. Ramsey RESET test and Breusch-Pagan / Cook-Weisberg test for heteroskedasticity

```
. regress realgdp faid dpriv dtrade sav gov t_dummy

      Source |       SS       df       MS              Number of obs =      31
-------------+------------------------------           F(  6,    24) =  174.19
       Model |  3.9354e+10     6  6.5590e+09           Prob > F      =  0.0000
    Residual |   903688984    24  37653707.7           R-squared     =  0.9776
-------------+------------------------------           Adj R-squared =  0.9719
       Total |  4.0258e+10    30  1.3419e+09           Root MSE      =  6136.3

------------------------------------------------------------------------------
     realgdp |      Coef.   Std. Err.      t    P>|t|     [95% Conf. Interval]
-------------+----------------------------------------------------------------
        faid |  -237.6299   397.1118    -0.60   0.555    -1057.228    581.9686
       dpriv |  -1304.504   954.3429    -1.37   0.184    -3274.171    665.1634
      dtrade |   456.4154   394.6635     1.16   0.259      -358.13    1270.961
         sav |  -1193.048   376.5366    -3.17   0.004    -1970.181   -415.9143
         gov |   2812.797   113.3887    24.81   0.000     2578.775     3046.82
     t_dummy |  -7922.488   3910.852    -2.03   0.054    -15994.09    149.1138
       _cons |   34774.58   5056.345     6.88   0.000      24338.8    45210.37
------------------------------------------------------------------------------

. tsset
        time variable:  years, 1981 to 2012
                delta:  1 unit

. estat ovtest

Ramsey RESET test using powers of the fitted values of realgdp
       Ho:  model has no omitted variables
                 F(3, 21) =     11.55
                 Prob > F =      0.0001

. estat hettest

Breusch-Pagan / Cook-Weisberg test for heteroskedasticity
         Ho: Constant variance
         Variables: fitted values of realgdp

         chi2(1)      =     0.07
         Prob > chi2  =   0.7955
```

www.ingramcontent.com/pod-product-compliance
Lightning Source LLC
La Vergne TN
LVHW102228300926
849160LV00005B/66